WHEN
LOVE
IS
LOST

WHEN

OVE

IS

OST

Donald J. Tyrell

WORD BOOKS,
PUBLISHER
Waco, Texas

WHEN LOVE IS LOST

Printed in the United States of America
Library of Congress catalog card number: 75-170915

This work is dedicated to all those
who have taught us to love

Contents

Preface

THIS IS a book that deals with normal personality growth, its challenges, the obstacles to such growth, and a technique that has been found to facilitate it. The author's basic assumption is that man needs to love even more than to be loved, that his true potential develops only in an atmosphere of love and trust, and that the refusal to reach out to others at the risk of rejection is one of the main obstacles to realizing his potential. Basically, the author seems to say, the human being is meant to love and be loved. But in growing up he incurs failures which uncover his weaknesses so that he meets rejection, real or imagined. Blaming himself for his shortcomings, he yet defends himself against other people's censure and resents his critics for forcing him to defend himself. In his rebellion, feeling condemned already, he may go on doing the very things for which he can expect punishment and rejection. His fear of being found out now adds to the pressure so that he feels threatened by everyone he meets. He can no longer love or trust others and begins to have a permanent sense of alienation that makes him try to flatter and placate people or to fight and overpower them, depending on what he feels is more effective at the time.

To free him for normal growth, the author insists, a man must break out of this vicious circle by confronting himself as he appears to others and as he really is. When he sees himself in the mirror of a group of people to whom he has opened himself, he discovers himself anew. Since the group accepts him as he is and loves him now that they know him, he is freed from the fear of rejection and can in turn love and accept them. Whenever a man breaks through his defenses and shows himself to others with all his failures and weaknesses, he risks rejection. If he finds acceptance instead of censure in the encounter group, if he finds love instead of anger, he will be free to love in turn, free to grow, free now to rule himself because he is no longer afraid that in so doing he is playing the enemy's game.

Every type of therapy, every systematic attempt to help others in their troubles and difficulties, is based on the therapist's basic convictions about the nature of man and his society. If a therapist is convinced that civilization has restrained and suppressed man's basic biological urges and so driven him into neurosis (as Freud holds), he will try to lift the repressions and help the patient to find the best possible compromise that will bring satisfaction yet be acceptable in the social world he has to live in. If, on the other hand, the therapist feels with Carl Rogers that man is basically good and will grow to his full potentiality if only he can recognize his true feelings and follow them, he will try to reflect these feelings in the counseling session and help the client to come to terms with them. Both types of therapy, in common with many others of the same vintage, aim to help troubled man by throwing him a lifeline while therapist or counselor remains safely ashore, secure in his professional status. Whether anonymous observer (in psychoanalysis) or faithful mirror (as in client-centered counseling) the therapist or counselor always remains apart from the problems that trouble those seeking aid, aloof from those he is trying to help.

In recent years, it has been objected that this kind of therapeutic relationship reduces the patient to a supplicant and elevates the therapist to a role of godlike omniscience. In an attempt to apply a corrective, behavior therapy approaches the patient as a subject who has acquired a socially undesirable set of conditioned reflexes and sets about providing more appropriate ones. The therapist becomes a social engineer who owes his best efforts to society rather than to an individual and so feels he is justified in doing his job impersonally.

None of these approaches does justice to the human being who needs to love and be loved if he is to have a motive for change. Significantly, behavior therapy works best with children and psychotics, that is, when human responsibility and freedom is either not yet achieved or is severely restricted, and when the therapist has the power to punish undesirable and "reinforce" or reward desirable behavior. In the last analysis, every adult is responsible for his own growth and progress. Even when he is painfully aware of the obstacles in his way, he wants to find out how to overcome them, what to do to resume his development, rather than being trained in more desirable or more acceptable behavior patterns. A man does not want to be manipulated, nor does he want to be observed or have his feelings reflected by an impersonal bystander. He wants to feel at home with others, wants to give and receive love and trust. Such mutual acceptance does not come about by one-way communication; it is the fruit of openhearted give and take.

For this reason, many therapists today try to meet anyone coming for help on such a give-and-take basis, preferably by having them join a therapy group. The participants are instructed to meet each other on the level of human experience, trusting each other to take the expression of genuine feelings in the right spirit, talking openly without fear of censure or rejection in a group of which the therapist is a member, vulnerable as they are, trusting others as they do. While such groups do operate on a truly human level, results are often long delayed because there is not time enough to devote to any given individual or his problems. In addition, it may happen that group members use the same direct approach with family, friends, and acquaintances in the mistaken notion that "honesty" can dispense with tact. This is certain to lead to grief in daily life where other people's feelings have to be considered.

What is new in the encounter-disclosure technique is that it is not group therapy in the accepted sense in which each member reacts equally to every other member of the group, at least in theory. In the technique described in this book, one particular individual confronts the group and everyone else concentrates on him, reacts to him and his problems, suffers with him if he is hard pressed, rejoices with him when he at last breaks through the barriers he has built up himself. This concentration on one individual has the effect of showing him that he matters to the group—matters individually to every individual. The very fact that everybody in the group is willing to stay with him, however long such a marathon session may take, that everybody tries to help him with his hang-ups and offers him understanding and friendship, is extraordinarily convincing. No matter how understanding and helpful an individual therapist, he cannot take the place of all the other people a man has met and contended with, and make up for their indifference. But when a whole group of people show their concern it is difficult for a man to hold out and easy to become convinced that he belongs and is accepted.

There are, of course, risks in this kind of disclosure. Not every member of the group may be discreet at all times. No matter how much emphasis is put on discretion or how insistent the therapist is that indiscriminate disclosure outside the group may be harmful, one or the other group member may be inclined to gossip, or he may be so enthusiastic about what the sessions have done for him that he mentions things out of context which may create an altogether false impression. This risk can be minimized by careful instruction, but it is a risk that has to be shared by every member of the group, including the therapist. There are other difficulties also, for instance, the effect of confrontation on particularly sensitive individuals, etc. All these problems are discussed in the last chapter.

Altogether, this little book deserves to be read and pondered.

MAGDA B. ARNOLD, Ph.D.
Loyola University, Chicago

Foreword

ONE OF the purposes of psychology is to bring harmony among the many theories concerning why man is the way he is. It also gives us criteria by which we can say with some degree of certitude that one interpretation of man is more adequate than another.

The understanding of the formation and development of the human personality is still incomplete. We must continue to search in this field, for ignorance and confusion manifest themselves boldly. While the methods of psychology are precise in the study of sensory processes, abnormal research, and pathology, we find them deficient and often sterile when they are applied to the human person. The behavior of sick and anxious people, of neurotic and desperate laboratory rats rather than the study of the healthy *human* personality serves as the basis for much personality theory that strives not so much to cure illnesses as to teach us how to live as intelligent, free, and responsible human beings. This lack of positive emphasis is seen in the fact that there are so many studies of criminals and so few of law-abiders; so many of fear and so few of courage; it is the reason we know so much of hostility and so little of affection, so much of man's blindness and so little of his hopes.

What then should be our approach for understanding the normal, healthy personality? We must somehow broaden the horizons of science without sacrificing its evident accomplishments in the interests of man's search to relate to himself, to others, and to God.

My understanding of the human person is closely related to my profession of the Christian message. Christ's double imperative, to love God and to love my neighbor as myself, lies at the heart of my approach to psychotherapy. I am convinced that we find perfection in the process of becoming persons only through living with and for each other. We see in Jesus the model who emptied himself of the prestige of divinity to meet us on our own level (Phil. 2:6–11). God's total disclosure of himself through the Incarnation was a risk that led him to death on a cross—naked, abandoned, and alone. It is such love that communicates the truth that will set us free.

This book has evolved from my own personal development, and from my search for a therapy more consistent with my convictions about the human person. Chapter 1 introduces us to the challenge of love by clarifying those convictions. Chapters 2 and 3 discuss the difficulties which a man meets as he searches to find himself and relate to others. In Chapter 4 we are confronted with the implications of our basic option to live for power or for love. The final chapter is more personal, detailing the results of my own growth which have led to a mode of psychotherapy based on the principles of the previous chapters.

While I take full responsibility for the contents of the book, I could never have done it alone. I have learned so much from my patients, my friends, my teachers and especially from my wife, Barbara, who continues to support me with her love in my often anxious, but always beautiful encounters with love. I could not begin to list the authors whose writings have influenced me. I would like to single out Dr. Magda B. Arnold for her patient assistance when I was a graduate student, her many hours of valuable consultation during my years of practice and her unfailing encouragement to me in my quest for self-understanding. I hold her as a dear and truly unforgettable friend.

Of the many others who have taken the risk to help me discover myself and understand my work, there are two who are especially responsible for this book—Jim Heisig and Bede Smith. They have struggled many hours with me in several drafts of this work, writing, correcting, editing, clarifying, confronting, challenging. They did this because they love me, and for this I am truly grateful. If our readers more deeply realize the possibility of love, then we have been worth it.

So the little prince tamed the fox. And when the hour of his departure drew near—

"Ah," said the fox, "I shall cry."

"It's your own fault," said the little prince. "I never wished you any sort of harm; but you wanted me to tame you . . ."

"Yes, that is so," said the fox.

"But now you are going to cry!" said the little prince.

"Yes, that is so," said the fox.

"Then it has done you no good at all!"

"It has done me good," said the fox. "Because of the color of the wheat fields." And then he added:

"Go and look again at the roses. You will understand now that yours is unique in all the world. Then come back to say goodbye to me, and I will make you a present of a secret." . . .

And he went back to meet the fox.

"Goodbye," he said.

"Goodbye," said the fox. "And now here is my secret, a very simple secret: It is only with the heart that one can see rightly; what is essential is invisible to the eye."

"What is essential is invisible to the eye," the little prince repeated, so that he would be sure to remember.

"It is the time you have wasted for your rose that makes your rose so important."

"It is the time I have wasted for my rose—" said the little prince so that he would be sure to remember.

"Men have forgotten this truth," said the fox. "But you must not forget it. You become responsible, forever, for what you have tamed. You are responsible for your rose . . ."

"I am responsible for my rose," the little prince repeated, so that he would be sure to remember.

1

The Challenge to Love

WHO AM I? WHAT SHOULD I DO?

No matter who a human being is, no matter what limitations have been imposed on him by society, no matter what the restrictions of his physical nature, there are two questions he must inevitably put to himself: Who am I? and What should I do?

The second question cannot be answered without some knowledge of the first, and the first is a mere pipedream if not translated into the second. The disordered and aimless activity of contemporary society witnesses to a confused inability to offer answers to these questions. Man tends to avoid the challenges of everyday living that might help him come to understand himself. Although he recognizes that meaning of self is found only in relation to others, he appears helpless to achieve those relationships. He fails to commit himself to others because he first fails to admit the impact he has on those about him.

How a man behaves is a reflection of what he values, and his values in turn tell us who he is. However, if

19

men judge one another *merely* in terms of external behavior, they are doomed to a superficial way of life, to
the fleeting satisfaction of shallow interaction. A man
may command proper and conforming respect from
his peers without ever facing the basic self-encounter
of "Who am I?" He will try to deny his own self-
awareness because he has been warned that he cannot
cope with it, and as a result, he finds that his dealings
with other people keep him at a distance and serve only
to harden his confusion into conviction. At times such
a man may pester people to the point of driving them
away, when he is really pleading with them to come
close to him. Conversely, if others seek to know him,
he becomes tense and afraid that they might find out
what he himself doesn't know—who he really is. That
a man will fear self-knowledge, that ignorance will
cripple his personal growth and insulate him from growing with his fellow man, is tragic. It is no wonder that
the time comes when he finds himself alone and
naked, sitting on top of the dung-heap of life and
wondering, like Job, "What have I done?"

Searching for Something More

Today, more than ever before, man is rebelling
against relationships based on the exigencies and pressures of environment rather than on free choice. People
are demanding choice, individuality, and responsibility
in their relations. But when faced with this burden,
they often become fearful and withdraw. It is indeed a
terrifying experience to be faced with the possibility of
love: the more freedom, the more responsibility, and the
more restrictions on that freedom. Those who wish to

avoid the constrictions of choosing must also avoid love itself, for love is a commitment involving the ever present risk of rejection. Many lack the courage to risk being rejected by others and find themselves paralyzed by fear. They are afraid to be accepted in love and afraid to accept others because, at the bottom of it all, they are afraid to accept themselves.

Some men flee into sensuality in a self-defeating attempt to understand love but this syndrome only weakens their concern for self-knowledge and growth. Love is a blind leap that risks ending in nothingness. Moreover, if one loves another with his *entire* being, he risks rejection of no less than that entire being. And because many are unwilling to undergo the adventure of such a feeble hope—fearing that they are ultimately unlovable—they end up as hedonists making the pleasure of safety the criterion for their behavior: if it is safe, it is good. Sexuality often follows this path and manifests the attempt to get involved without making a commitment. "If it is safe and we both enjoy it, and it doesn't harm anyone else, why not?" This ethic is negative and severely dehumanizing because a self-satisfied slavery has replaced a liberating influence on others. A life without risk is either distorted or monotonous. The person who fears failure so much that he refuses to love distorts not only his own personality but also that of others around him.

The disturbance today surrounding adolescent behavior, and the mutual distrust between adults and teenagers, is symptomatic of a culture suffering from a lack of communication. The claim of many adults to be disgusted with the adolescent masks a deep-seated fear, the fear of what they have given birth to. Adult society must live with the adolescent subculture it has produced, whose rebellion stands in judgment against much of what adult society represents. The teen partially understands the adult world but runs from it because he fears rejection. Rather than make a positive commitment, he foolishly seeks to be accepted by his peers by avoiding the risk of communication with his elders.

It is easy enough to turn in repulsion from anything we fear. It is easy enough to say that sex maniacs and drug addicts ought to be locked up, and then feel secure that such precautions have bettered man's condition by alleviating some evil. It is much more difficult, however, to become involved with the people who threaten us, to recognize our role in their deprivation. It is deceptively comforting to blame a child's maladaptive behavior on the crowd that he hangs around with, without ever questioning what produced that crowd. Our culture has harvested a generation of adolescents that are so preoccupied with rejecting their elders that they can hardly accept themselves. They are so frightened by society that they can only rebel against it. My experience has been that many teenagers respond to questions of self-identity by disassociating themselves from the adult community. Nevertheless, adolescents tend to be closer to confronting the questions "Who am I?" and "What should I do?" than adults who have displaced such concerns with the ephemeral details of daily chores.

Although man's highest needs and desires are independent of his environment, his concerns and primordial questions differ from culture to culture. An Eskimo's lifestyle is successful if he survives the onslaught of his surroundings, because his energy is almost totally concentrated on staying alive from season to season. Our country, too, began in the struggles of a people for survival in the taming of a new land. Yet at the very dawn of that history, the Constitution of the United States supplied a heritage for those who would no longer have to be preoccupied with mere survival. It speaks of inalienable rights, the dignity of man, his relationship with others based on love towards his fellowman and towards God. To their misfortune, people blessed with such a legacy have lacked the wisdom to realize that their task is more difficult than fighting the elements and tilling the soil. And now that material comfort has alleviated the battle to survive, the next step has become more difficult because it calls us beyond the security of physical well-being to the creative insecurity of a new struggle.

WHERE AM I GOING? HOW DO I GET THERE?

In 1929 a serious economic depression came upon our country and lasted for several years. During this time, the average man did well to keep himself and his family alive. World War II followed close at the heels of the economic disaster and again men were forced literally to fight for their lives. But after the war came a period of affluence when the values men held dear and reached out for seemed to have been achieved. Living standards exceeded anything previously imagined and people clung desperately to them as a safeguard against having to repeat their bitter past which so few had survived. The children raised in this affluence assumed that it had always existed and that things had never been different —and indeed for them they never had. For the child who saw two or three cars in the garage and whose "needs" were based on superficial wants or passing styles, it was difficult to understand what it was to work for a new car or an education.

The commitment of one generation to survival loses its meaning when the next generation has no trouble surviving and insists on goals beyond those that inspired their parents. It is little surprise that parents do not appreciate this change in viewpoint, since material possessions held such a value in their own lives. But what happens when material security is no longer a goal but a fact of life—where does one aim then? Those adults who spent their energies competing with society for economic betterment are at a loss to appreciate the adolescent's question: Where to from here? And what is more, the question suppressed in their own past under the worries of survival springs back anew: Who am I? Those who have spent themselves to insure material comfort have done well. But their perspective is rendered obsolete by their children. Where should they go? What should they do? Who are they? A teenage patient once showed me this section from her diary:

"I'm no one's most important. And I have no one most important to me. It's a bad way for me to live. Loveless living is loneliness on top of aloneness, a waste of time. The lack of love enslaves your mind, and is joyless—and on top of that, just plain irritating." It is sad that this expression of anguish is not atypical. But we can see in its confrontation with the questions "Who am I?" and "What shall I do?" something of beauty also: her willingness to risk to find the love relationship, to expose and reveal her self by choice rather than by coercion.

Great sensitivity is required of a human being who is willing to be open, to reveal his feelings and to face criticism in order to enter into a positive relationship with another person. A person who tries to get close to another always experiences a tense hope that his risk will not result in rejection. His willingness to trust first himself and then others, so as to come to know himself, is an involvement that cannot be taken lightly; but, unfortunately, it is one that is often discarded as irrelevant in today's pace.

The Fear of Human Involvement

Frank, a twenty-three-year-old, recently revealed in a therapy session before a group of his peers certain aspects of his behavior that he had been unable to tell me in two years of private consultation. He ended his monologue of very unpretty behavior with the statement: "I can't go on hiding any more. I want so much for people to accept me, to like me, to love me, but I cannot in fairness ask you people to love only part of me. Now, you will probably all reject me. But there may be one of you that will not, and if there is only one in this group who can still tolerate me, so that I will have the experience of knowing a human being who accepts me as I am, then it will give me the courage to go on and try to be myself with other people. I hope I can give up this kind of behavior, because I would finally have a reason to do so." The fact that not one person in the group of ten did reject him was, to Frank, a new experience. He could now stop fighting himself. He could now stop attempting to deny the bad self and was no longer afraid to be the good self. An era in his life was over. He no longer had to live a façade; a confrontation with himself had taken effect. He had torn away the mask and encountered other human beings as he was. Frank had exposed himself with the risk of rejection, and for the first time in his life others were able to accept him for what he truly was.

It would be an overdramatization to say that Frank's behavior changed from that moment on, for the habits of hiding are not so easily uprooted. He still had much more growing to do. He still had much more self-understanding to accomplish, and he still had to face the fact that his commitment to others was a new phase in the continuing process of becoming a person. The submission of his personality and his exposure to the group, however, was a plea for love, not for power—a plea for acceptance as he was, not as he tried to make others think he was. It was a plea to help him change and a plea for a reason to change. In an honest meeting with other human beings Frank was making an attempt to reveal his deception of self and others, with no guarantee that he would be accepted. He was really saying to the group, "I want to love you and I want you to love me. But for this relationship to be accomplished, we must be honest with one another." No longer did he fear involvement with the group, he welcomed it. No longer did his fear of rejection by the group inhibit his openness. Frank had gained enough respect for the group and for himself to confess himself openly and honestly.

Spectator or Participant?

My own realization of the need for total honesty, openness, confrontation, and commitment of oneself to another has evolved over several years. There have been critical experiences in my life and in my practice of clinical psychology that have produced the evolution of my thinking and behavior in dealing with others.

Several years ago a man came to see me because his wife was prostituting herself and forcing their children not only to witness her activities, but to participate in them. As he told the story, it became evident that, if he were telling the truth, the children should be removed from their mother and placed with him. In the state where the man lived, this was a difficult thing to do, but I thought I would meet my professional responsibility by finding a lawyer for the man to support his case in court. One day the man came into my office and said, "I can't take it any more. Something has to be done. I just cannot go on living in this situation without doing something. And you *have* to help me. You must do something." My advice to him reflected the priority of my own concerns. In the first stages of building a practice at the time and trying to build up a reputation of successful treatment, I really didn't want to get involved in this kind of situation. Instead, I proposed several clichés to the man, including the necessity of abiding by legal sanctions, being patient and praying to God. He left the office and a few hours later put twenty-seven stab wounds in his wife. He is now doing a life sentence in prison. The children are with their maternal grandmother and apparently leading disrupted lives. This occurred in part, I believe, because I failed to get involved as a person, because I failed to take the risk of commitment to another human being, because I failed to respond beyond the bounds of my professional responsibility—because I failed to love.

Most modes of psychotherapy demand a commitment on the part of the patient, but require only under-standing and empathy on the part of the therapist. The patient is asked to explore, to ramble, to intel-lectually regurgitate experiences from his own life. But he knows nothing about the therapist's life. The patient is asked to spell out all his problems, all of his idiosyn-cracies, all of his immoralities, all of his mistakes, all of his negative relationships with people. He is asked to expose himself to the therapist, but the therapist makes no such commitment to him.

It seems likely that this one-way involvement is re-sponsible for many psychotherapeutic failures. In a traditional analytic approach, a patient may be asked to see the doctor several times a week for three to five years and spend hundreds of hours verbally exposing himself, but never really knowing the therapist, as the patient barters self-revelation for the psychologist's pro-fessional knowledge. It is almost as if love between them were not desirable. If the therapist understands the patient, that should suffice. The patient is encouraged to feel a trusting dependence on the therapist, but the therapist may not express human love or become in-volved with the patient on an emotional basis. The effective therapist is generally considered to be a de-tached, understanding spectator.

Over a period of years, it became increasingly ap-parent to me that this kind of relationship could be a dehumanizing experience to the patient and could inhibit his growth. The disappointment many psychotherapists have had in dealing with patients is generally not pub-licly announced, but the fact that so many psychi-atrists and psychologists have ended up on the other

side of the couch themselves may be testimony to a
basic, although unwitting, dishonesty in their relationships with their patients.

There have been many recent attempts to deal with
people effectively. The Cursillo movement in Catholic
retreats involves long sessions where adults attempt to
expose themselves to each other, intellectively and
emotionally. These have met with a fair amount of
success, particularly when the leaders of the group were
willing to make the same commitment. Synanon groups
working with drug addicts are similarly oriented and
apparently meet with considerable success. Much group
therapy work done by professionals testifies to the fact
that success or lack of it depends not only on the skill
of the therapist but on the commitment or exposure of
himself that he is willing to make to the group. This
means nothing less than a willingness to disclose all of
one's feelings without qualification or exception.

The Courage to Participate

I recall an occasion when I was involved with a
teenage group as part of a team consisting of people from
various professions who spent the weekend in intimate
dialogue with the boys. One of the leaders was a Catholic
priest who represented to me many of the unfavorable
aspects of the priesthood. He struck me as a flighty, unmanly, uncommitted person. One of the teenagers
asked him at one point, "We're supposed to say anything we want? Is that right?"

The priest replied, "Yes, let your feelings out."

"Even if it might upset you or offend you, you want
me to tell you what I think of you?"

The priest, with some skepticism in his voice, said, "Yes, I would want to hear it."

"Well, I think you're an asshole."

The priest doubled up like a boxer who had just been dealt a right hook. I expected his legs to collapse. But he gathered his balance and said to the boy, "I am sorry you feel this way. I wish I were the kind of guy you would like to imitate. I wish I were the kind of man you wanted to grow up to be like. But I am glad you said what you said, because you believe it. And, I care about you."

The boy broke into tears, ran up to the priest, put his arms around him and responded to the commitment of love. This man who had looked so wishy-washy had shown his deep concern and openness. He had responded to an attack with love and broken through the barrier. The boy's defense that he so wanted to have destroyed came down and provided an opportunity of growth for both of them.

DISCLOSURE AND CONFRONTATION

Experience has taught me that any attempt at a two-way commitment of love demands an exposure of personalities to the extent that it is useful for both persons. Some rather dramatic cases illustrate this.

I received a telephone call about two years ago from a widow who claimed that her twenty-year-old son, Arthur, was contemplating suicide because he felt he could not, in conscience, go to Viet Nam. He was in the army and was due to be flown overseas in a week. Obviously, he could not afford the luxury of a therapeutic approach involving weekly visits for several years. Either intervention would have to be immediate, responding to the crisis, or I would have to tell this woman that there was nothing I could do. I agreed to see the young man on a Friday evening. When he came into the office, I told him that I had nothing scheduled until Monday morning and that these appointments could be cancelled if necessary. I told him he was free to leave my office at this point; but that if he chose to stay, before he left he was going to know who I was and I was going to know who he was. I told him that if he chose to stay I would hold him to that choice and not allow him to leave. He decided to go through with it.

First I attempted to get him to discuss his problems; but what followed was an hour of rationalized word-games in which Arthur spewed out the answers he hoped I wanted. In fact, he even said once, "Haven't I told you everything you want to hear?" Arthur obviously was unwilling or unable to expose himself on an intel-lectual level.

Moving to another level of exposure, I confronted him with his artificiality. I called him a fake, a phony, and told him that he was expecting me to do something I couldn't do. I asked him what he wanted of me and kept repeating that question until he began to get angry. He quickly recovered, however, and retreated to the safety of sterile conversation. It became apparent, as time went on, that he was also unwilling, or perhaps even unable, to disclose himself emotionally. At this point I asked whether he wished to leave or if he really wanted to understand himself. I asked him how far he was willing to go to obtain such understanding. Again, he chose to stay.

Since intellectual and emotional disclosure was inhibited, I explained that physical denuding, as a symbol of deeper exposure, might reveal what he was really hiding. I asked him to remove his clothes. Arthur removed his clothes but not without some fear. It was an attempt to return him to a state of childlike helplessness in order to prove that it is possible to be defenseless and yet not be harmed. I questioned him constantly: "How do you feel? . . . Are you afraid I am going to sexually attack you? . . . Do you think I am going to hit you?" I attempted to imagine what fantasies might be going through his head and verbalized these fantasies to him. He denied any such fears. When I walked over to him, he began to cry. It was not the crying of an adult, but of a helpless infant who kept saying over and over, "Please help me. Please help me. I want to grow up." I asked him to look into my eyes and tell me what he saw. He said, "I see viciousness and anger. I see a man I cannot trust. I see a man who's going to hurt me." I asked him to look more closely and told him to cut out the dramatic nonsense. What Arthur saw was a reflection of himself. I asked him to try and remember when *he* really wanted to be vicious, when *he* really wanted to attack, when *he* really wanted to hurt. And I asked him to tell me whatever came into his mind at this point. This is the story he told:

"My parents have been divorced for several years. My father was an alcoholic, and I remember when I was quite young, maybe eight or ten, that my father was beating my mother, and my mother called for help.

I was the only one home. I went to help her. I wanted to make my father stop beating her. When I asked him to stop, he said, 'If you weren't so small and helpless, you'd be getting it, too.' I hid in the corner, covered my face, and tried not to watch. Crying, I asked him to stop hurting my mother. I cried some more. He kicked at me and left the house. I cried and cried. I told myself afterwards that it was a bad dream, that it didn't happen. Later my mother told me that it was a bad dream and that it didn't happen but I knew it had. I haven't thought about this in years. Why do you make me bring it up? Why do you?"

Arthur had become so angry it looked as if he were going to attack me. I just looked at him, and then reached out and held him. "I'm not your father. I care about you." With that, Arthur wept bitterly.

I told him of my own difficulties in growing up that were germane to his. The rest of the story is anticlimax. As we talked for several hours to put the pieces together, it became apparent that Arthur made his identity depend on his being helpless. For if he grew up and became strong, he would have to attack his father. He would have to hurt and risk being hurt. He felt free enough now to tell me about dropping out of school, failing in his job, and finally ending up in the army. The army insisted that he was a man and was old enough to fight, so he was being sent to Viet Nam, perhaps to kill. That possibility had stirred up the original anxiety of his feelings toward his father. He would not have faced this anxiety if I had not been willing to expose it through confrontation at whatever level was necessary.

It is interesting that not once during the early part of the session was Viet Nam mentioned. Arthur claimed that he still would not go to Viet Nam because he felt that the war was immoral. But instead of killing himself, or running away, or committing a crime, as he had originally planned to do, he turned himself in to the army authorities and refused to fight in Viet Nam. His mother called a few days later and told me, "My son has been depressed for at least five to seven years and I haven't known why. It is the first time in all these years since he began high school that I have seen his spirits lifted. He really looks like he has finally arrived. Arthur is now talking about returning to college and completing his education when he is out of the service. I think he has something to live for even though he is still confused."

Finding a Common Ground

It seems to me that a responsible therapist must meet the person where he is in fact, rather than where the therapist wants him to be. If the therapist is to involve himself in a person's process of becoming, he must begin with that person's present state and grow with him, rather than simply hold out a seemingly unattainable goal of maturity.

In a VA hospital several years ago, a forty-five-year-old man used to sit in my lap and I would feed him bread dipped in milk. After three months he was able to go to the cafeteria with the rest of the patients. This incident is significant when one considers that he had been unable to do so for fifteen years. Again, this was a case of meeting a person where he was—in this case in an infantile, primitive, demanding, oral stage.

In a similar case with a seventeen-year-old boy whom I'd seen for several months, I asked him what he really wanted to do at a particular moment. He said, "I'd like to sit on your lap." I allowed him to do so. His thumb went into his mouth. He started sucking and rocking like a baby. I asked him how he felt. "Like all my troubles are gone," he said. "Like you're going to take care of me and help me grow up." It was the first enthusiasm I had seen in this boy in many sessions. But when he went home and told his parents of how kind the doctor had been and that the nice doctor had let him sit on his lap, the parents were upset and withdrew the child from treatment. Several months later he had a psychotic break and has been hospitalized in a state hospital since that time.

I have no way of knowing whether I would have been successful with the boy if the parents had permitted me to continue working with him. But I strongly suspect that here, as elsewhere, external inhibitions and cultural taboos have blocked true personality growth and prevented healthy development.

The apparent, but I believe necessary, extremism of another case further clarifies the point. Several months ago I conducted a disclosure-confrontation marathon session with three married couples, my wife, and another therapist. One of the women on the session, Lucille, who was middle-aged, had come with the freely chosen commitment to share herself completely with the group in the hope of salvaging a failing marriage. It soon became apparent that she was involving the group in her own

comfortable pseudo-problems and that there was another level of exposure, deeper than the intellectual, to
be reached in order to discover what she was hiding.
When the co-therapist began to question her honesty
and to share his personal feelings towards her, spontaneously employing language she considered foul,
Lucille became upset. But she shielded her anger by
retreating to her defense of being a "nice" lady and
objecting that the language being used was quite unnecessary. When he did not stop, she began to scold
him strongly, in a stern and almost motherly fashion.

I walked over and stood in front of her, my arms
extended wide. "Do whatever you feel like doing," I
invited her.

Giving herself time to gather her wits, she repeated
the command. Then she stood up and, taking my head
into her hand and drawing me close to her, kissed me
on the forehead.

"Judas!" I shouted at her. "That wasn't real!"

With that she breathed heavily through her teeth
and slapped me three times across the face.

"That," I told her calmly, "was real."

Lucille went into a rage. She began to scratch at me,
kick, bite and do everything possible to destroy me for
reflecting something inside of her that she had been trying to conceal. Her language got coarse, hardly what
we would have expected from the nice, cultured lady
who had been bantering about with us a few minutes
before.

Under the impact of the confrontation she struggled
and fought with me to exhaustion. As she collapsed to
the floor, she sighed deeply, her thoughts flowing freely.

"I never knew I had that inside of me. I really don't know who I am."

What she was coming to realize was that she was not as powerful as she had thought, that she had not in fact destroyed me, that her anger was not so powerful or dangerous with someone who had truly committed himself to her. My part in the confrontation had been to contain her in her anger, never to attack, but only to encourage her revelation of pent-up wrath. I turned to her and asked, "What do you want from me?"

Half with embarrassment, half with hope, she replied, "Can you accept me after all that?"

My response was not effusive, but an honest expression of my feelings at the moment: "I'm beginning to love you."

She broke down into tears and wept for several minutes.

After that Lucille turned to her husband, and, with refreshed perception, spoke quietly but sincerely to him, "The air smells so clean. Can you smell it? And everything is so quiet, so peaceful. You look so handsome. I'm sure I have never seen you like this before." She turned to me and reached out, tenderly putting her hand on my face. "Thank you for helping me with your beauty—and mine."

With renewed courage she began to talk to the group about herself and her marriage. It had been the second marriage for both Lucille and her husband, each having previously divorced out of an unhappy situation. Lucille told us her mother had arranged her first marriage and how angry at her mother this had made her, although she had thought that such anger was hardly befitting of a proper lady. (Lucille understood at once that I had caught her feelings towards her mother.) Her mother's marriage, similarly prearranged by the family, had ended unhappily, and Lucille now recognized that she was doomed to a second failure unless she owned up to her own feelings. To do so was made even more difficult for her since her first husband had been seeing other women, leaving her with a feeling of inferiority. She and her present husband, never having faced what the past had done to them, had thereby allowed it to control them unconsciously. They were forced to defend themselves from their feelings, and communications in their own marriage and in the family had eventually broken down.

After eight intensive hours, this part of the group session ended. When we returned to Lucille's husband later, she helped him to uncover his own feelings towards his past. But the main point here is that if I had supported this woman's defenses and been afraid to invite her to truly express herself, if I had walked away from her when she got violent, or attacked her so as to stifle her response, she would have retreated into immaturity again, a courteous but inwardly very dissatisfied person. At present this marriage is restored on new grounds. Although Lucille and her husband can look forward to more crises and pains, they have freed themselves from an enslaving and hidden store of feelings. They have opted for the commitment to honest communication which alone can transform those crises and pains into a source of growth rather than excuses for another dissatisfied divorce.

Comfort or Commitment

Drastic as the approach in the previous examples may appear, the fact remains that in a human relationship disclosure must take place if the relationship is to be meaningful. If we look about us and ask how many happy marriages we really know, how many communicative love relationships we have witnessed, most of us would be shocked at the small number. I submit that such marriages are so rare because one partner or the other is hiding something—something which perhaps the other person doesn't strictly have the right to know, but something which would lead to a fuller mutual knowledge and, consequently, a greater acceptance and love.

The ability to reach out by first reaching inward, to face ourselves as we really are because of the worth of another, is the basis of the love encounter. Two people must recognize each other as valuable: "I'm valuable and worthwhile; I have something to give. You are valuable and worthwhile and I want to give myself to you." How much more sensible this is than attempting to escape from ourselves by getting lost in a love relationship! This mutual judgment of value is, as the teenagers put it, the "real turn-on," not the turn-on of drugs or alcohol or sex or any of the other myriad escape mechanisms that engulf us.

To accept myself means to judge myself as worthwhile, whatever scars my past has left with me. Similarly, to accept someone else is to judge him, with his past, worthy of love and to make the commitment to grow with him, fully aware that mistakes will be made in the process. Clearly, I cannot achieve this sort of intimacy by myself. The difference between disclosure and exhibitionism, between confrontation and attack, is a critical one. It would be of no value to walk into a supermarket and reveal my innermost self to the sales girl. Rather, it is our intimate relationships with a few "significant others" which are the foundation for future relationships of varying degrees of intensity and revelation. We can get by in life, of course, by nurturing a set of convenient defense mechanisms whose validity we do not question. But by revealing only part of ourselves to others while they only partially expose themselves to us, we cheat ourselves and them by having so little to do with them. On the other hand, we can face life with understanding, realizing that growth must come from inside and not be left to mere environmental pressures. As we reveal the depths of our true selves to others we can create the opportunity to know them and through this knowledge continue to grow in love relationships. Though this alternative is neither comfortable nor secure because it involves risks that are as serious as any human being can face, I am convinced of its worth.

A very practical question we must all learn to deal with is the extent to which we can reveal ourselves in our personal relationships. It would be hazardous to expose ourselves at random or without preparation to others who may not be ready for the revelation. The depth of commitment in each particular situation must be assessed, based on the criteria of self-value, the value of the other person, and the potential depth of the relationship involved. In some situations, self-disclosure can be dangerous if not foolish. We must face the fact that there are individuals who might use such confidences to their own advantage. Each person who makes a decision to disclose himself freely must do so not because he is too naïve to realize the risk he assumes but because he feels the risk is justified. If another person cares about me and wants to trust me and I feel the same way towards him, then I must decide whether a genuine love relationship is worth the risk involved. And if I am unwilling or unable to take that risk, human dignity demands that I confront the other person with my reluctance and the reasons for it.

At a recent weekend session we had a group of senior boys, acquaintances from the same high school. One of them, perhaps the most friendly of the entire group and superficially the best adjusted, seemed to be doing a great deal of listening with no verbal, emotional, or physical signs of identifying with the other participants. During each encounter, he sat back passively with apparent interest but showing no signs of acceptance.

We took a short break, and when the group came back, Charlie said, "I want to be next." By this time the group had achieved a certain state of solidarity, a cohesiveness that would not have allowed Charlie to escape once he had chosen to be honest. He was immediately confronted with the lack of trust his "close friends" felt towards him and the fact that they enjoyed his company only on a very shallow level. Jolted by this heavy blow to his pride, he maneuvered every which way in order to persuade the group to trust him. The group refused the tactic, saying to him in effect, "We have given trust. We want to know you. We want you to tell us about yourself." What he went on to relate was vague and safe and the group was aware, at once, that it lacked depth and the honesty they had felt with the others who had already spoken. One of the boys spoke up, "I feel cheated. I have exposed myself to you. I told you I loved you and meant it and you're unwilling to reveal yourself to me. I want to get to know you as a person and you're cheating me by failing to tell me who you are." It was interesting to watch Charlie's defenses of habit—defenses of protection, of alienation and isolation. But eventually the group's honesty with their questions and their demonstrations of trust and anger broke through Charlie's shell. In this circumscribed group, with the impact of the others on him, he was able to cry out, pleading for the chance to grow up.

Once Charlie realized that the group did trust him and wanted his trust in return, the rest followed more easily. He began by telling us that when he was three years old, his father died. Apparently, he was very fond of his father. He remembered stories from his mother of how kind and loving and openly demonstrative of affection his father was. When his mother remarried a few years later, the boy readily received his stepfather, who was also kind and loving. But in spite of this, he was still captured by the strong attachment to his real father. With a great deal of emotion, Charlie continued to explain, "I guess I never grew up beyond that point. My greatest need now is to have friends. I will do anything to have friends. I will do anything to make people like me. I will do anything I can for people because I want so desperately to have them like me."

At this point I stepped in. Confronting him with his arrested development, I suggested that he had been unable to give in any human relationship because of being deprived of his father. This had produced a fear that any trust given to another person might result in the loss of that person.

Charlie then blurted out, "If I really tell you people about me, will you still like me? Can we still be friends?"

I pointed out that he really did not have any friends except at a three-year-old level. "How old do you really feel?" I asked him.

"You're right," he admitted. "I feel like a three-year-old."

"Is that what you really want to be? If so, the group probably could accept this. But they would have to treat you as a three-year-old, and people do not have a mature communication with a three-year-old. A three-year-old can *take* but has little to *give*," I pointed out.

The session continued with the exposure of his infantilism, and the group showed him that he drained people for his own satisfaction. Even the fact that he was considered by many adults to be a "cute boy" was spoiled for him when someone in the group commented, "No wonder adults like you. How much of a threat can a three-year-old be?"

This kind of confrontation may seem very cruel at a distance, but after it had continued for about four hours, it was beautiful to see Charlie growing up, abandoning his infantilism, and finally declaring to the group, "I want to be eighteen. I want to love you as an eighteen-year-old. Would you be willing to take the chance to love me as an eighteen-year-old?"

The group response was positive, real, and emotional. Charlie faced the risk and the group faced it with him. He remarked after the session, "I didn't know it was possible to grow fifteen years in a few hours."

Any confrontation, if it is to be meaningful, has to be a true dialogue between equals. If we insist in our relationships on adopting the parent-child model, we are playing a hazardous game with life. By dealing with people only as father to child, I might maintain my own protective image but destroy the possibility of real communication. Many things about myself which I disclose are difficult. There are many things that I wish I had not done. There are many encounters with moral problems in which I was not the victor. There have been many self-defeating, self-demeaning, and dehumanizing episodes in my life which I wish had not occurred. These I am often called upon to confess to friends, to myself, and to God. Only in learning to share have I come to know that love has not been lost—and it is this knowledge I want most to share with others.

2

Frustration: The Gift of Growth

WHEN GOALS are blocked, the resulting conflict and, often, frustration can be detrimental to growth. In reaching out to people around us, impelled by the need to communicate and share ourselves on the highest levels of human activity, we may experience constricting barriers. Empty conversation may obscure intended goals and postpone growth. Our efforts to reveal and share ourselves with others are especially visible in our handling of sex, anger and fear. But the very conflicts and frustrations experienced there can become means to human fulfillment and growth.

THE ESCAPE FROM SELF

Man's lifetime search to know more about himself and his world is defined by the goals he sets for himself, many of which he may never reach. Goals that fulfill certain aspects of his nature may limit or cancel others. Often his quest for fulfillment is spiced with failure. A personal judgment of wrongdoing or fear that he will be hurt if he shares the knowledge of his failures may cause him to hide them. The result can only be confusion in himself and a deep-felt disharmony with others. When failures are acknowledged, their damaging consequences can often be corrected. The person who denies them, however, can, at best, persuade himself to live without clear awareness. But he will pay the cost—the gradual disruption of his own life and impoverishment of the lives of those around him. As he infects himself by hiding, he spreads the contagion, and the creative human capacity for open, honest, shared love turns sour.

We Choose What We Get

Not long ago, the parents of a boy whom I had been treating came to my office for help. Brad and Cecilia had arranged for their son to see me after they had found him using drugs. Now it was their turn, as their son, encouraged by his own progress, urged them to join a group session. As Cecilia said in an initial interview, she wanted to change herself and her marriage. And both parents wanted to understand how they might have been part of the cause for their son's difficulties.

When Cecilia came to speak about herself on the session, however, she chose to hide her feelings. Instead, she accused her husband of insensitivity and of making a mess of their promising married life. She blamed Brad for their family problems and claimed that the only reason she was not applying for a divorce was that it would disrupt the lives of the children. Rather than remain firm to her commitment of total and unqualified openness to the group, Cecilia backed down and retreated into herself. Unwilling to allow the group to probe deeper and perhaps help her discover the source of her fears, she told us to leave her alone. It was soon apparent that she felt no real need to change herself and that the only reason she had really come was to expose the immaturity of her husband. She insisted that the therapists had conned the group into thinking that all the fault lay with her.

Without forcing her, I tried to help Cecilia get beneath these superficial defenses, but she chose not to. Although she had already revealed something of her past, she had become anxious about unveiling her true feelings, particularly feelings toward her father who had frequently beaten his children, had tried to sexually molest her and had carried on affairs with other women. To protect herself from the anger she felt towards her father, Cecilia idealized him to others, rationalizing that any faults he had were caused by an illness and eventually convincing herself of this false image. She had been hurt, but she was unwilling to part with her constructs of the past and express honest feelings about her father and herself.

Later in the session Brad spoke, but in a quite different manner. He confronted Cecilia with her immaturity and responded honestly to the group's confrontation of him. He told her frankly that if they didn't love each other, it would be best for the sake of the children to break up the marriage rather than live a lie and spread the damage to them. Cecilia refused to respond, however, and left the session. Brad decided to remain with her, hoping that his continued honesty may some day free her. Their boy has since returned to drugs and delinquent behavior. Unfortunately, Cecilia refused to see me again and seems destined to remain enclosed within her own immature fears. She will infect her children with them until such time as she can find it in herself to admit her own dishonesty in perpetuating the false image she has created of herself and her past life.

But We Get What We Choose

Whenever we cover over the sores of our lives and live on appearances, we create an obstacle to our self-acceptance that in turn causes us to doubt our acceptability to others. We are forever goaded by the question: Would they accept me, if they knew . . . ? The fear of a negative answer forces us to pull the veil even tighter. Instead of *being* humble we try to *appear* humble, instead of having self-understanding we are satisfied by the appearance of insight. We read the cover flap of a book and talk about its contents. We hear the words of a conversation and pretend to understand without listening. We tell people we have sympathy for their tribulations when, in fact, we are grateful that it is they and not we who suffer. The appearances of success become the destructive and disruptive avoidance of self-knowledge. In the effort to obtain a calculated response, we say what is opportune, even insincere, dishonest, and unreal. The hidden wound does not heal but only festers under the skin. And rather than risk the exposure to the open air that might allow it to heal, it grows and becomes even more difficult to conceal.

The dishonest person must calculate what he says.

Defensive against values he does not understand, he is unable to seek new values, new challenges, new adventures. He feels trapped, fearing that he will fall apart if his own dishonesty and pretenses are confronted. But though he knows he is miserable, he either doesn't know what to do or is unwilling to take the risk. Life is a treadmill on which he frantically stays alive because he pitiably fears death. He constantly runs from himself. To defend himself from the possible confrontation, he must attribute to others the responsibility for his own self-inflicted wounds. He is suspicious of others and projects on them malefactions so that he can deal with them without meeting himself.

Reversing the Vicious Circle

By putting a premium on acceptable neuroses, our society encourages us to abandon ourselves to the delusion that it is all right to be mildly neurotic. Plagued with anxiety, tensions, and unrealistic fears, we spend huge sums of money on research, medicine, and psychotherapy for ills that are often the effect of our own irresponsibility. By learning to live with guilt feelings, we in fact avoid the guilt that is the failure to meet responsibility. We gladly fill the coffers of physicians, churches, and "charity" institutions who falsely claim to absolve us without challenging us with our responsibility.

Guilt is not an emotion as we would like to believe, but the result of a violation of responsibility toward ourselves or others. When we fail in a responsibility, we experience feelings of shame, embarrassment, and fear. Inherently these feelings contain an element of untruth. If we can wade through them to find the real guilt, which may be quite concealed by the feelings, we can be confronted with our responsibility and then have the possibility to change. In therapy I always try to help a person find the *lies* in his life rather than focus on the *discomfort* that results from these lies. To the extent that he can know himself, he can begin to do something about his condition. But as long as he denies that self-knowledge, he is powerless to remedy his illness.

As a man continues to hide and, in the process, to deny guilt, he will become increasingly maladjusted. Heaping lie upon lie, he will probably learn to hate himself and become aggressive toward anyone who reminds him of his deceit. A dishonest man cannot tolerate an honest one and will often attack him viciously to protect his own vulnerability.

It Hurts to Walk on Stones

If we could but love ourselves, with our failures, and their results, we could begin to be honest with others. If we loved ourselves, we would demand to know ourselves as we really are. We could stop hiding and, instead of damaging ourselves, we might begin to accept the responsibility of our strength. It is an ironic tribute to man's sense of justice that he instinctively attacks what he hates. The fact that man hates himself as the result of his lack of self-knowledge unfortunately gives him no choice but to be self-destructive. Having repressed or denied accurate self-knowledge, he is afraid to move in this direction or that direction, and he finds that a choice based on fear is no choice. He is coerced, not free. But the fearful consequence of a life of hiding is neurosis and derangement in both an intrapersonal and an interpersonal sense. It is the destruction of the relationship between man and man. For we attack what we hate and we suppress what we fear. It is the dishonest person who fears himself and others who will seek revenge not only on himself but on other people around him.

To reverse the cycle of dishonesty and self-punishment means that we must give up immaturity. It means that we must be willing to risk exposing our wounds, to risk loving ourselves—even the horrible dark side which we would like to pretend is not ours—and it demands the revelation of ourselves to others and the willingness to be honest with them.

Freedom begins with honesty, but so much of life resists our efforts at it. When I was working at a VA hospital a few years ago, I met a patient who insisted that he was Marilyn Monroe. I used to make rounds every day and call him by his real name. He was mute and unresponsive. One morning I addressed him, "Good morning, Miss Monroe." He looked up and said, "You're getting to be as crazy as I am." While entering into the pattern of hiding may be amusing, it is no solution for our dishonesty or that of another person.

Inevitably, as we begin the search to discover ourselves, we will meet blocks and obstacles. Honesty does not require that every urge be followed or every emotion expressed. In fact, the failures and frustrations that occur can be part of the search. It is one thing to hide them and quite another to see them as opportunities for growth. That we cannot grow without risking and encountering them is a common enough experience. For instance, a student can choose to study late at night and deny his bodily need for sleep, or he can decide that sleep is more important than his coming examinations. Even if there is an honest mistake in the choice, there won't be anxiety over it because the deprivation was consciously accepted. At worst, the student will pay the price of his error and learn something for future decisions. It is only if he deludes himself—by lying or disguising the facts—that anxiety can result. If he deceives himself, whether knowingly or not, and makes an incorrect choice, he will be forced to multiply the deception by blaming some external factor for his error. When he defends himself in this way, he abandons his development and takes an avenue of escape that can eventually supplant self-knowledge with neurosis, psychosis, or physical illness. As a man escapes from the responsibility of living with the results of his choices and omits integrating them into his personality, he will travel further from the central concerns of his life. The environment will choke him rather than permit him to embrace it. His actions will become self-defeating; his life will descend into a desperate and often violent struggle to hide from himself and others the mistakes that could give character to his personality and encouragement to his growth.

A man may have a cocktail or two before dinner because it relaxes him physically, reduces his tension, makes him feel better. But if he continues imbibing to the point of drunkenness, then he may have sated his immediate physiological and emotional needs at the expense of his total personality. The amount of damage will depend on the immediate and long-range effects. To get drunk occasionally is not as harmful as to be a chronic alcoholic. One can eat to excess occasionally, with little overall effect, but to overeat continually would result in obesity with all its physical and psychic complications.

To hide from the consequences of our behavior is to foster anxiety; and the more we hide and the less we realize why we are afraid, the more we become enmeshed in that anxiety. Anxiety is not an unfounded fear, it is fear of something because of our *inability* to face the true source of those feelings or because of our *choice* not to face the source. The result is that we become increasingly anxious as we flail about seeking an explanation that we can accept comfortably—in other words, an explanation that is false. I have all too often seen people who have clear evidence of the origin of their anxieties, but who totally deny any negative feelings because they refuse to assume the obligation either of dealing with their origin or of modifying their behavior.

The control of behavior is not, as Freud has suggested, simply a matter of organizing our emotional impulses. It depends, rather, on guiding our understanding towards goals and values in such a way that an appropriate emotion for the particular situation is produced. Emotions form a link between the physical and intellective levels of man. On the one hand, it is clear that a healthy physical makeup favors emotional stability, but on the other, it is apparent every emotional response is a response to something that is perceived and evaluated as an object to be desired or to be avoided. An emotion is a normal, uncontrollable response to judgment, and the behavior associated with an emotion will be modified only if one further judges that such a change is for the better.

This way of viewing emotions has implications for the suggestion common to many psychiatrists and psychologists that patients who are angry ought to go pound on sand, let off steam, and drain their systems of the feelings of anger. But once an emotion is aroused, it more easily increases than decreases in intensity. An angry man becomes even more angry once he begins to discharge his anger into some form of behavior, since the emotion will reinforce the judgment that "this potentially harmful object should be destroyed or harmed." Chopping wood or beating a punching bag *apparently* drains emotions; it is more likely that an interval is provided during which understanding and judgments are reorganized.

The well-known advice of counting to ten before giving in to anger provides the same kind of chance to view the situation differently, to reappraise it before launching into action. An immediate explosion of anger may only reinforce the first interpretation. In the time we are counting, we may gain perspective or a better understanding of the situation. We are not so much frantically tightening screws on a pressure lid as trying to determine what caused the pressure in the first place and how best to deal with it. In counseling people, I never suggest that they "drain" emotion, but rather recommend that they try to find out just what makes them feel the way they do and judge what might be the consequence of their behavior.

THE COST OF HIDING

As we noted before, self-understanding is vital. We are continually challenged to accept that insight and use it constructively in pursuit of our goals. We need to realize that insight can serve both growth and the escape from growth; a man may always choose to hide and use a convenient selection of insights to assist him in that choice.

We cannot have stability of emotional life until we achieve a degree of intellectual understanding of it. This may be a very difficult task. For instance, the "angry young man" may resist the insight into the real source of his anger while becoming quite sophisticated in his understanding of the external evils he is protesting. If, for example, he is angry at one of his parents, the conflict between that emotion and the judgment of love—or the ideal that parents are to be loved and respected—may blind him to the understanding that would help him face the object of his anger realistically. Until that blindspot is removed, the young man will remain angry while his emotion is irrationally displaced onto teachers, police, or other "safe" authority figures. The way to modify the emotion is to clarify understanding, not to ignore the emotion or imprison it within oneself.

I remember a professional marriage counselor who was a member of a group session that lasted six consecutive days. He talked for several hours, uninterrupted, and at one point broke his thoughts to blurt out at me, "Don't you know that if you let me continue I may try to kill you?" I assured him I was aware of the risk and encouraged him to continue.

Later he did attack me, violently, and the day after that had to be hospitalized because he had reached the point where he was becoming dangerous to the group. He remained in the hospital five days, remarking to me at one point: "If I had known you really loved me and that I wouldn't have killed you, I would have seen you years ago." Incidentally, over the years he had consulted several professionals and each time, rather than receiving help, he had been advised to hold in his hostilities. Our group confrontation was a messy therapeutic scene, but the fact is that until someone could care enough for this man to reach out and accept him *as he was*, he could not grow beyond his hostilities. Until he could disclose himself as he was, he continued to multiply frustrations in his own life. Jourard explains:

> One of the reasons less healthy personalities are so self-conscious, so deliberate in their choice of word and action before others, is that they dread letting something slip out that truly expresses their being, something which will get them into trouble. They are, as it were, idolaters of the state of artificial grace known as "staying out of trouble." In fact, they have sold their souls and possibilities for a good but false name.[1]

Here was the wretchedness in this man's life. He didn't want to be a fake, but he couldn't find anyone who would help him *share* his negative feelings. His anger at me and at the group was a protection against the fear that he was not acceptable as he was, and consequently, his growth was arrested. Though he wanted to take the risk of being authentic, of really disclosing himself, he had been so well trained in suspicion that he had to test my authenticity and that of the group.

This risk of exposing ourselves to another is dramatically expressed in the correspondence between Eldridge Cleaver and his lawyer, Beverly Axelrod, while he was in Folsom Prison. She writes:

> What an awesome thing it is to feel one's self on the verge of the possibility of really knowing another person. Can it ever happen? I'm not sure. I don't know that any people can really strip themselves that naked in front of each other, we're so filled with fears of rejection and pretenses that we can't tell whether we're being fraudulent or our real selves.[2]

Cleaver answers her letter:

> The reason two people are reluctant to really strip themselves naked in front of each other is because in doing so they make themselves vulnerable and give enormous power over themselves one to the other. How awful! How deadly, how catastrophically they can hurt each other, rack and ruin each other forever! How often indeed, they end up by inflicting pains and torment upon each other. Better to maintain shallow affairs; that way the scars are not too deep, no blood is hacked from the soul.[3]

As long as a person is reaching his goals without being unduly frustrated, his emotions are positive. But it is a part of life that man does not always reach his goals, and this incites negative emotions. He feels frustrated as he struggles towards his goals and realizes the discrepancy between what he is doing and what he ought to be doing. There is at least an intuitive realization that he ought to have coped with his environment more effectively.

That he can be frustrated is one of man's mixed blessings. Lower animals aren't frustrated as much as higher animals because they are not aware of any discrepancy. But only man can have tragedy in his life because only man can be conscious of the frustration of unfulfilled possibility. Only man can be aware of what he "could have been." The plant grows if the minerals in the ground are sufficient and if it has the proper amount of light and water, but it can hardly experience dissatisfaction about deficiencies in its environment. It merely withers and dies. In contrast, man can choose his goals and so is in the unique position of also having them blocked and frustrated. Condemned to reach for goals that he cannot always attain, he continually expands his horizon as his personality grows. In the process he maintains his uniqueness, his distinction as an individual among other persons. But this growth is a becoming with, a growing into the community of other men. One may rebel against this community and escape from it because he feels stifled by the broader group, but this is always done at the risk of alienation from that community.

Growing with Others or Decaying Alone

This, then, is one of man's greatest personal struggles: to maintain cohesion with other men and at the same time to insure his individuality. The hippie phenomenon is particularly interesting in that it has often turned in upon itself, by the ironical sacrifice of community for individuality. The hippies have largely set themselves apart from the mainstream of the American people, in protest against the dishonesty of the American way of life; but so strong is their own need for social living that they have come to form their own communities. Frequently those communities produce disenchantment. In part their members were led to assume the very life-style they abhorred, viz., artificiality, in order to be able to express themselves. To be "real," many of them used drugs excessively, and the result was often less real than what they were running from. The use of such artificial turn-ons is no accident; its tragedy is that it is self-defeating and only witnesses to artificiality as a substitute for more adequate values.

On the other hand, the conservative strain in society, the "Establishment," is often as dishonest as those who reject it. It uses different techniques for hiding. By isolating the "dangerous" elements of society—drug addicts, homosexuals, the mentally ill, minority groups—the Establishment shields itself from them lest it recognize in itself these very dangers. We can read of a stabbing in the paper and feel safely removed from it, until we look inside ourselves and see the same potentiality there. Through a heavy network of laws, conservative society protects itself from its destructive potentialities, but it is another thing to pretend that such forces exist only "out there" and not also inside ourselves. As a group, the conservatives want to be left alone, isolated from the problems their way of life has produced, removed from the mistakes that breathe in the real bodies of real people in *their* community. Just as the Romans once built a solid but static empire that classified all outsiders as barbarians and thus fell into the corruption of isolationism, contemporary affluent man can build a mighty fortress about himself only to find that he has enclosed the very frustration he is trying to wall out. The upkeep of such a life is inconvenient in the extreme: it involves the loss of self by over-protection, loss of life by self-sufficiency, and a weakening of understanding by narrowing the universe down to what is manageable, agreeable, and nonconfronting. Where, then, does the real frustration lie? On which side of the wall is the loneliness, the fear, the irresponsibility?

DEVELOPMENT AND CONSCIOUS FRUSTRATION

Ralph, a seventeen-year-old high school senior with a strong B average, was referred to me some time ago. Although he knew that he would disappoint his parents' dreams if he didn't continue his education, he insisted that he would drop out of school in his final semester before graduation. He told me later, "If only once my parents, or someone, had told me to go to school so I could learn, learn about myself and about people, learn who I was and who other people are. But, no! All anyone keeps saying to me is, 'Go to school to make a good living.' What's the point of a good living if you don't even know who you are? I've tried to talk to my parents about this and all they can say is, 'Well, you're young and you don't understand.' Well, I don't want to understand that kind of life. Why can't they understand that? Why can't they listen to me?"

When I talked to the parents and told them that the boy was seeking and demanding honest communication with them, that he would run from them unless they would openly talk with him, their reply was, "Look, we didn't come here to have you tell us how to live. Just get the boy back into school." I read them the following short passage from Jourard:

> I have an informed suspicion, one consistent with a number of lines of experimental data that we do have, that *I* am a strong determiner of how open and trusting the other fellow is going to get. I suspect that he will become as open, trusting and vulnerable as I am willing to be with him. If I want him to be maximally open, then I have to be prepared to be maximally open. If I want him to be only half-open, then I will only get half-open. If I want him to be maximally open, but I keep myself fully closed off, peeking at him through chinks in my own armor, trying to manipulate him from a distance, then in due time he will discover that I am not in the same mode; and he will then put his armor back on and peer at me through chinks in it, and he will try to manipulate me.[4]

Ralph was removed from psychotherapy; the parents accused me of being incompetent. Soon he quit school and joined the army, running from the impossible goal of true communication. Both the boy and his parents will live with frustration until true and open communication can be established.

Frustration, conscious or unconscious, is something we will inevitably meet in the search to become our-

selves. Frustration is *unconscious* either if we are un-
aware of it because we do not recognize it for what it is,
or if we do not accept the limitations that our nature and
environment impose on us. It is even possible that a
therapist can unwittingly encourage a false self-image
in someone and drive him into this sort of unconscious
frustration which inhibits growth and only generates
anxiety. The contrasting cases of two university students
may help to clarify what we mean.

Truth Hurts More When You Run

A few years ago in a graduate-level course in abnormal psychology I had two students who showed
particular interest in my work, each producing in
class at a B-plus level. One of them volunteered to help
me with a research project. Because of his interest and
apparent ability, I encouraged him to continue studying
psychology, offering him my assistance if he would ever
need it. I had no idea that he was secretly struggling to
keep up with my expectations of him in his papers and
exams. The truth of the matter was that he felt inadequate in the face of my hopes for him. His grades began
to fall lower and lower until he was failing most of his
other courses, while somehow managing to keep me
hoodwinked. He continually postponed his work on the
research project and kept promising to have it completed
in the near future. Fortunately, some of his classmates
told me what was happening, and I was able to discuss
the matter frankly with him and admit that the fault
was largely mine. But rather than face himself, he
dropped out of school entirely and broke off all contact

with me and his classmates, even though we had invited him to participate in a later marathon session for which he had previously shown much enthusiasm.

The other student responded quite differently to a similar confrontation. Not only did he not run from the situation, but freely chose to face his feelings and self-deception. He has gone on in graduate school and is holding a teaching position at present, having secured a much more accurate, but no less growth-orientated understanding of himself.

The possibility of such hidden anxieties points to the importance of an adequate self-image as the basis for a self-ideal. In stubbornly denying himself an authentic self-image, the first student was condemned to sink far below reasonable expectations and is still beset with latent frustrations. By comparison, the second student has accepted his limitations and dealt intelligently with the unconscious frustration situation.

Conscious frustration, by contrast, occurs at the level of conscious judgment—a judgment made in full awareness of the barrier that stands between an individual and his goal. Although conscious frustration is a maladjustment when viewed from the narrow perspective of a particular personal goal, it is necessary for total personal growth. The elimination of certain goals may be required to prevent even greater frustration. Take the obvious instance of the child who wants to watch TV, read a book, and play ball all at the same time. The frustration of not choosing one goal in preference to the others would be far worse than consciously opting to exclude two of the possibilities. Likewise, a student may wish to complete his college education, get married and raise a family, and be a playboy all at once. The judgment that all three are possible simultaneously is superficially and intrinsically inconsistent; one or more of the goals will have to be eliminated in service of the others. Merely to coexist peacefully with such conflict is a choice against freedom. As William James once remarked, "Not to choose in the face of a situation demanding choice is actually to choose." A young man who respects his girl friend will probably not become sexually involved with her until he is in a position both to accept the responsibilities that go with belonging to her and to assume the commitments for the future which the sexual expression of love entails. For if he really cares about her, he will not take the foolish chance of hurting her, no matter how much pleasure he has to deny himself for her sake. The commitment, involving evident frustration, will then be to each other's value, not to each other's pleasure.

In personal development, long-range goals should predominate, and this assumes what I have called "conscious frustration." Despite the negative connotation of the term, it is not only a very positive step but is often a necessary deterrent to worse frustrations. Even a moment's reflection will reveal that efficient daily living requires it constantly.

In addition to the limitations conditioned by personal deficiencies, there are also a multitude of possible barriers created by the environment. A man may have all the intellectual ability to go to medical school but not the economic wherewithal. Or, he may have both but still be refused admission because of crowded university conditions. Or again, he may have the intelligence and money and be admitted, but still be unable to go because of an illness in the family that makes it necessary for him to remain at home to help. The list of such environmental barriers could go on and on.

Although the personal decision involved in overcoming such barriers might appear good cause for pessimism, they can be exhilarating. Producing a worthwhile piece of art means more to the artist because of the hard work put into it. To have faced a difficult situation and mastered it is far more rewarding than to have achieved a goal effortlessly.

This appreciation of the value of struggle in one's search provides needed insight into a serious problem within contemporary society. The affluent parent is gradually coming to realize the hazards of giving his children all the things he didn't have. Parents who so indulge their children, making the assumption that it is the *things* themselves that are satisfying rather than the process of *striving* after them, are inoculating their children's lives against the spirit of adventure and the possibility of growth.

Many of the over-thirty generation were taught that maturity is an accomplishment to be achieved and then preserved, when in fact there is no such thing as *maturity*—only the process of *maturing*. Parents who feel that they have "arrived," educate their children to become like them; many such parents use their children to convince themselves of their own worth—"If I can produce a successful child, I can't be so bad." But in the failure to reveal to their children the struggles of their own life searches, parents cheat them of an accurate picture of adulthood and perhaps force them to greater mistakes and a less conscious search than their own has been.

CONFLICT AND SELF-UNDERSTANDING

There is a bit of the mountain climber in all of us. Even though there may be a breathtaking view from the top of the mountain, that would hardly seem to be sufficient reason for climbing instead of using a helicopter until we realize that human growth seems to require the self-respect that comes from removing obstacles and overcoming frustration. In our country millions of dollars are spent every year doing just that in recreational sports—especially those that require skill, effort and endurance.

The tired executive may sign a membership to the local health club and engage in gruelling physical exercises one or two nights a week. The reason involves more than his physique, however, particularly since the rest of the week usually proves to be the undoing of all the physical benefit. It rather serves the purpose of offering a self-imposed challenge, an obstacle to be overcome, all without any real risk.

Most of us do not need to go out of our way to find conflict situations; life is all too generous with them. What is important for us is to decide how to respond. The fear incited by a mad dog on the loose is self-protective, but the fear of imaginary dangers is unhealthy. To be told we can live without any fear at all is untrue, for learning to live with uncertainty and to meet it intelligently is necessary for growth. We can understand ourselves only if we understand what is happening to us. Knowledge of what has happened outside, in the shifting external situation, isn't enough; self-knowledge is a prelude to an authentic self-image that can be shared with others. How do we resolve the conflict of openness against hiding, love against hatred, growth against decline, and dynamism against stagnation?

Backing into the Wall

There are several methods for dealing with particular conflict situations. One can, first of all, *retreat from the situation* and deny that the goal has any importance for him, labeling it "sour grapes." He can use defense mechanisms. He may even incur physical illness to avoid the necessity of dealing with the conflict. In short, he can either hide from others or lie to himself.

Any conflict situation involves some threat to the security of the individual because there is question as to whether or not the barrier can be overcome. If the goal is not reached, the person may have to blame himself. If he sets out to do something and cannot accomplish it, he will obviously be discouraged with himself and even though he rationalizes excuses, the discouragement stubbornly remains. Moreover, others may become disenchanted with him for promising what cannot be fulfilled, and express their feelings in antagonism.

The threat of not obtaining the goal can be overwhelming and cause deep disturbances in the personality. As values are threatened, we reassess our positions. Faced with the possibility of aspiring to something that we cannot obtain, we may become anxious, panic, and run away. In a situation like this, we tend to rely on principles of behavior, and if these principles are adaptive, we will either find another goal, surmount the obstacle, or accept the fact that we cannot attain it. If we choose maladaptive principles, however, as the proverbial fox did, and use defense mechanisms—create excuses or blame the failure on others or the environment—our behavior will be maladaptive and there will be an inevitable disturbance in personality functioning.

By defense mechanisms we mean certain automatic, often unconscious techniques for protecting the self-image when it is threatened. All are means for hiding. Typically they do not alter the situation, but merely relieve the immediate anxiety by concealing or distorting the threat. The person who fails to get a promotion at work may realistically evaluate the reasons and work to change himself or the particular circumstances that prohibited the promotion. But if he relies on defense mechanisms, he may blame the boss, tell himself and others that he was cheated, or accuse his wife of making it impossible for him. He will not be able to cope with the situation successfully. Adequate striving toward the goal will cease or be inhibited. Antagonism and physiological stress will replace personality growth. If he continues to operate on the basis of such principles, he will come to mistrust himself and others. In this mistrust he may seek out persons who support him in his position, but in the end he will pay the price for his dishonesty.

Finding a World to Fit Me

When we find that we have wasted our efforts in striving for unattainable goals, we can gain encouragement either by denying the reality of the situation or by denying the value of the goal. In either case, we are likely to retreat to an environment that will not challenge us. If a person is convinced that he is a dull and immoral person, he will associate with a peer group whose members make the same kind of judgments about themselves. Such people remain aloof in their interpersonal relationships because all communication has become suspect. In spite of the fact that they may travel in packs with people who share their own frustrations, they become isolated and lonely because their frustrations are unconscious. In failing to trust themselves and others, they live in constant dread that someone may break through their shell and find out who they really are. Their answer to the fundamental question "Who am I?" is negative and discouraging. They have lost self-love and with it the ability to share themselves with others.

A person will deal with conflict on the basis of his life-experience and his self-image. In the case of the gang delinquent, for example, there is a disturbance in the self-image which yields negative value-standards and a sort of general moral renunciation. Somewhere along the line, a person who identifies with the social fringe has been taught that he is second-rate. He accepts this self-image in his dealings with the world. A parent who constantly confronts his child with the fact that he is no good will sooner or later find the child reinforcing that belief at every opportunity. If a person *totally* abandons himself as worthless, he will either damage the world by maladaptive behavior or damage himself by ceasing to grow or even committing suicide.

When a man has learned from experience that he is easily harmed by his environment, conflict situations may translate their tensions into pervasive anxieties or phobias—a fear of getting hurt, and the like. If he has learned that tensions mean that he is about to fail, he may reduce the conflict by running or by defending himself. For example, a little known fact about Adolph Hitler is that he had only one testicle. One wonders if this organic inferiority—which must have tarnished his masculine ideal—was in part responsible for a type of paranoid psychosis. Did he perhaps feel so inferior that he attempted to destroy the world by trying to prove to himself that he really was a man? Certainly, his concentration on the super-race must have been related to his self-judgment of personal inadequacy and his psychotic defenses against this judgment. As long as Hitler was able to deceive himself and others regarding his own power, he was able to avoid his underlying fears of powerlessness.

Using Your Head on a Brick Wall

Besides responding to a barrier by retreating from it, it is possible to *meet the conflict situation head-on.* If the barrier is completely unyielding, frustration brings anxiety. A teenager who was referred to me some time ago was exposing himself physically in front of the little girls of the neighborhood. I tried to show him that he was crying for help, but that his self-defeating behavior pattern was frightening to people around him and only kept them at a distance—that his problem would only be deepened, not solved, if he ended up in jail.

As he soon discovered, the problem was really very simple. He had a late puberty and his parents were too rigid in their moral principles to help him understand his anxiety over his newly-discovered sexuality. He was afraid of meeting girls his own age, socially as well as sexually. He felt inadequate, but reckoned that if he waved his penis around enough, someone would pay attention to it and tell him what to do with it. Because little girls were neither a social nor a sexual threat to his immaturity, he became exhibitionistic in front of them. As soon as he came to understand this, he was able to adjust his behavior accordingly and has not exposed himself since. It has been over three years now; he is dating and doing quite well socially. If he had kept hitting against the barrier to communication without proper understanding, he would have drifted into deeper and deeper frustration.

If there is the slightest hope of overcoming a particular barrier, even though repeated attempts may be necessary, and if the goal is sufficiently worthwhile, then such struggle has meaning and the personality will grow. We allow ourselves to be frustrated as long as there is some hope of reaching a goal we consider valuable enough. That progress in science and medicine is particularly dependent upon perseverance is well known. Though scientists work against apparently insurmountable odds they are not harmfully frustrated because there is a realistic hope of a breakthrough. We need only think of the vast amount of scientific resources expended before the first man stepped onto the moon, or of the painstakingly slow search for the secret of cancer. The scientific reports of successful experiments are enough to fill huge libraries but all the libraries of the world could not contain the accounts of their failures.

Running in Circles Brings You Back to the Same Place

A third way of dealing with conflict is to *circumvent the barrier,* to go around it to attain the goal. Often teenagers, faced with the fact that their parents are threatened by them, really have to work around their parents' anxiety. Usually the parents will use their power position to deny their problems and anxieties. I know of one father who, as each of his four sons reached puberty, found some excuse to have them drop their pants so that he could beat them on the buttocks with a two-by-four. His repeated refusal to face his own sexual immaturity, of which this act was indicative, eventually caused each of the sons to retire to a safe distance from him. One retreated into psychosis; one is at present fornicating and feeding his problems with narcotics. A third joined the ministry to escape his father; and the fourth, who accepted the fact that his father is a man with severe problems who can be accepted the way he is, simply moved out, married, and became an adequate person in spite of the trauma.

A defense mechanism may be useful at times because it can allow us to pull ourselves together before moving ahead. To rationalize may help us feel adequate for the time being, until we discover more stable grounds on which to establish self-worth. If we feel that acceptance within a group depends upon physical prowess, we may rationalize about it until we find it unnecessary to do so. Or if lack of physical prowess is so obvious as to make rationalizing about it impossible, we can circumvent the barrier by finding other aspects of personality that would achieve the goal of acceptance. Defense mechanisms can provide valuable time to reappraise the situation and find alternate routes toward a goal.

Second Choice May Be Best

Instead of going around the barrier by alternate routes, we may *choose alternate goals* that are as satisfying as the original goal. This is particularly common when our inherent limitations block the goal. Even when the alternate goal is not as satisfying as the original, as long as it can be accepted without necessitating the misuse of defense mechanisms, it will serve the integration of the personality.

A few years ago it was considered a horrible thing for a man to leave the ministry. Now this has become more acceptable; in fact, positive aspects are beginning to be recognized. One young priest, after a long session with me not too long ago, decided in all honesty that he must leave the priesthood—perhaps to return someday, perhaps not. He knew he must investigate an alternative goal, the possibility of marriage, and the possibility of earning a living elsewhere than in the ministry. As he said himself, "I have to learn to live with myself. I recognize now that I am worthwhile and that I don't have to use the structure of a religious community to hide from myself." I consider the move a very positive one for this man, and I see it in no way detracting from his commitment to become a full person. Now I am not advocating that all priests or ministers leave their ministry, but it seems to me that each person must be permitted a faith that is an honest search for integrity and identity. To deny someone the freedom of this search is to deprive him of his humanness. For faith is what makes him human, if to be human is to search beyond his own limits and to transcend his experiences. Faith as a search demands total involvement, total commitment, and a willingness to travel the road of investigation in spite of the hazards along the way. Traveling along this road may call for the serious consideration of an alternative route, which need not indicate the surrender of the search.

Clearing the Fog

From the above, we see that three elements in the process of meeting conflicts are important if we are to avoid confusion: an understanding of ourselves, an understanding of the elements of the conflict situation, and an appreciation of the goals that are blocked. If we understand the elements of the situation, our behavior will be smoother.

The importance of both self-knowledge and knowledge of the environment cannot be overstressed. Knowledge of one of these and not the other may cause intolerable frustration and harm. If we know our environment, but do not know ourselves and our resources, we are not sure of what we can count on in meeting difficult situations. We may be frustrated and not know why. The tension in a conflict situation which we might effectively have used for learning will turn into neurotic anxiety. Instead of being tense, we will be fearful and not know the cause of our fear. And in our attempts to account for it, we may inappropriately attach it to something irrelevant where it would be useless in helping to handle the situation.

Harmful frustration occurs in a conflict situation only when inadequate solutions are being attempted. We can judge solutions to be inadequate if we lack knowledge of self or of the situation, or choose a poor solution because we are hiding. If we handle the conflict situation realistically in terms of what we bring to the situation, and if we take into account the demands of the environment, personality growth will continue. This obviously requires a good deal of doing. Socrates' injunction "Know thyself" has become no more easy for us than for those who trod the dusty paths of Athens.

3

Disclosure:
The Search for Self-Understanding

THE TWO questions "Who am I?" and "What should I do?" run a parallel course; the answers to each depend on the answers given to the other. What I think I should do influences who I think I am, and even more importantly, who I think I am suggests what I should do. But whether my self-awareness is correct or distorted, deep or shallow, the values I assimilate or reject will reflect their consistency with that awareness. This tendency for consistency between what I know and what I do is the direct expression of a man's tendency toward integration and wholeness.

As the person grows, values are absorbed or imposed from external sources through parents, teachers, and peers. Eventually, they must be personally understood and assimilated, if they are to be a mature and motivating force in life. Values critically interrelate the individual's self-image and self-ideal. When the evaluation process has attained some balance, they may in love be shared and communicated with another person.

VALUES AND THE PERSON

We have seen judgment on every level, from perception through emotions to intellectual judgments as the motivating force behind behavior. Values, as the objects of judgment, are also, therefore, determined by physical, emotional, and intellective factors. Preceding the decision in every choice situation there is an evaluation based on these factors. If I order a liverwurst sandwich instead of a banana split, it may be because I like the taste of liverwurst better (emotional basis) or because I consider it better for my health (intellectual basis). If I have been involved in a serious automobile accident, my attitude toward driving an automobile may be determined more by the emotional residue of that event than by an intellectual judgment about my driving ability.

As a man matures in his self-awareness, he is able to gauge his activities by values that have become a part of him and have been assimilated through reasoning or are consonant with it. If, then, he decides something on an emotional basis, he is at least aware of that component in his value system. Generally, a mature person is motivated by what he thinks rather than by what he feels. This does not mean that decisions based on feelings are in themselves wrong, but only that they must also be consistent with insight.

Even in the maladaptive personality, life is organized around a set of values. The values of the sensual hedonist, for example, cause him to subordinate higher values to lower, at the expense of harmonious personality functioning. Whether we agree with those values or not, they are present and give direction to his life, unifying his personality. A person always acts in a way he considers good for himself.

Frequently I ask people how they answer when their children ask, "Why should I be good?" It is disconcerting to hear the answers given, because so few of them indicate that the parents have responded according to the child's total personality. One typical answer, "So you will feel better," suggests that emotional or physiological satisfaction is sufficient reason for acting in a particular way. The teenager in the back seat of a car with his girl friend and a bottle of whiskey to keep him company does *feel good* at the time. It would be difficult to convince him to abstain from the activities he is likely contemplating on the basis of feeling better.

The Need for Values to Change

Five years ago, when I lacked the insight and courage to deal with people by making a total commitment to them, a fifteen-year-old high school sophomore was referred to me. Although quite intelligent, he was doing poorly in school, and also was having difficulty with his parents. At that time, I was still using what I later recognized as a selfish approach of remaining distant while collecting a fee for listening. I saw the boy once a week for several months. He made some improvement in behavior and his grades were a little better, but he still was not achieving to the maximum of his ability. There was considerable pressure from his parents to terminate therapy and eventually he chose to discontinue it completely.

He finished high school, but, after flunking out his first year in college, he returned again on his own for more therapy. He explained that he was dissatisfied with his lack of academic achievement and wanted to improve his grades. In a long session I confronted him with his own selfishness and immaturity and pointed out that he would have to deal with himself before there could be any concrete change in motivation or achievement. Feeling that I had calmed him and maneuvered him but that we had really been wasting each other's time, there seemed to be nothing to do but terminate the session. When I shared this feeling with him, he said, "Look, I know you like me, and that you genuinely care about me. I like you too. I've never been as free to talk with anyone as I have to talk to you. And because you care about me, I'm going to tell you something. I know the game I'm playing with my parents. I know I have a new car out in the parking lot that my parents just bought for me. I know what I'm doing and I like it. I realize that my behavior is an expression of anger towards my parents although I don't want to confront them directly. I like the rewards I am getting as they try to buy me. Because you are honest with me, I am telling you this. And what I really want from you is that you get off my back and leave me alone. When I really have the desire to change, I'll come back."

His apparent unwillingness to change was discouraging but I felt at the time that it was an honest expression of the boy's opinion. Over the next two years, during which we kept casual contact, I learned that he had flunked out of three more semesters of college at two different schools. Up to this point he had been successful and rather comfortable with his strategies and con games. But as he began to realize the lack of true success they were giving him, he became more uncomfortable with himself as well as with his failures. A year later he was back in my office. He said he had decided it was time to change. In a long session, much repressed anger came to the surface. He attacked me physically and attempted to seduce me sexually. At length he broke down in tears, honestly confessing his guilt and his fear that if he gave up the game there would be nothing left in the relationship between him and his parents. In his attempt to "feel good" he had been defeating himself until he realized the need to make commitments beyond immediate gratification. Convinced that his change in motivation is real, several people have helped him obtain admission to a small college on a one-semester trial. He has also sat down with his parents and dealt with them honestly. Now that he is better equipped to answer the questions "Who am I?" and "What should I do?" he has more self-confidence and is better able to relate and deal with the people in his life. The motivation to achieve beyond immediate gratification has enabled him to accept the demands that must be met in order for him to work at his full potential.

Another frequently encountered value standard is that "it's okay, if you don't get caught." This answer assumes that since whatever you can get away with is acceptable behavior, one's goal should be to avoid harm to oneself or to others. Teenage culture seems often to be moving in the direction of this type of social hedonism. It judges that if one does not get hurt and does not hurt others (measuring "hurt" on a very limited physiological basis) then the behavior is appropriate. And yet, much of teenage music reflects a yearning for more. Although many of their physiological needs are gratified through food, sex, or drugs, deeper emotional needs are starved. Unfortunately, they attempt to meet these emotional aches of loneliness, rejection, and the feeling of worthlessness through a secluded search in the same pleasure channels of more food, more sex, and more drugs. Growth is suffocated by the excess.

During the writing of this book, an interesting scene occurred below my third floor window. Outside in a grassy, sparsely wooded area some boys were playing baseball. Closer to the building in a small park a boy and a girl were sitting on a bench. Both of them, about fifteen or sixteen years old, were engaged in grappling embraces, film-screen kisses, and furtive touches. Just then two men walked by. The kids playing baseball waved to them, but the two lovers, embarrassed, pulled apart quickly and froze. Once the men had passed, the baseball game continued at its previous pace and so did the sex game. The difference in response between the two kids who were obviously "caught" as opposed to the baseball players who were simply observed, illustrates what I have been saying. The implications of an interrupted baseball game are potentially less damaging than those of the interrupted sex game. The teenagers must have been aware of their wrong behavior or they would not have stopped so abruptly when someone walked by.

Whatever values one adopts to answer the question

"What should I do?" have their effect in shaping the personality. But they have a real formative influence only when assimilated into personal conviction. Behavior based only on "feeling good" or "not getting caught" will hardly lead to personality growth.

THE ASSIMILATION OF VALUES

Before we are old enough to shape our own values, we accept the external standards imposed on us through parents and society. Whether these values are religious or humanistic, there comes a point when they must either be accepted or rejected by a personal decision. Only then do we answer our own question of "What should I do?" The answer need not be so individualistic that it contradicts the values of our parents or society, but it must be unique in answering our own questions and evaluation. Certainly we may choose to obey or disobey the standards imposed on us from without, but if we choose disobedience, it is all the more patent that personal choice is involved.

It is less easy to see that a choice *for* values held by other persons is also a positive choice even though no change in activity is involved. The adolescent boy who refuses to engage in heavy petting with a particular girl may act either from fear of "getting caught" by parents or in respect for the girl. Though there is no difference in the external behavior, there is a big difference in the values expressed. Fear of being caught and respect for another person are radically different *values*.

The child following certain dictates of parents either

in fear of punishment or of rejection by his parents will probably discard this value later. He will sense that his growth is being stifled through motives of fear based on external standards, and his awareness of the need for independence may even cause him to reject values that are good in themselves because they are imposed from without. Even though the infant and child are dependent and must abide by externally imposed values, the growing person is increasingly confronted with *his* question of "What am I to become?" His search for an answer implies the assimilation of values that affirm his individuality.

A person's self-image—his own answer to his self-directed question "Who am I?"—refers to the person as he is now, in the present. But as he looks to the future and asks himself, "What am I to become?" his answer describes his self-ideal. This picture of the self as it ought to become, as we have already shown, is just as important as the present image of oneself. When there is a discrepancy between the image and the ideal, unrest and tension is inevitable. Ideally, behavior serves to close the gap between ourselves as we are now and ourselves as we judge we ought to become. When this gap is realistic in its proportions, the tension it creates inspires growth, energy is released and resources are made available to spur us to maturity. But if the gap is too great something must "give."

Tension in Growth

We have been taught, especially in Western culture, that tension is to be avoided at all cost. Tension, anxiety, and frustration are often considered evils to be cured by the magic of medicine, the power of prayer, or the soporifics of psychology. Quite the opposite attitude should, in fact, be encouraged. We should welcome tension and we should welcome frustration. We should welcome barriers, for it is in overcoming them and in reducing tension in the process that the balance of the personality is kept intact while growth is allowed to continue.

Just as anxiety is the sign that we are afraid of something and should discover what it is, tension is the sign that we need to express ourselves in creative action. I recall one priest in a group marathon who was simply unable to show any strong emotion. He intellectualized and categorized all of his life activities. He admitted that he was unhappy but could only express his state of mind in words. The group kept pressuring him to let go with his feelings. One of them, more disturbed than the rest by the priest's apparent inability to do so, was becoming pale, extremely agitated, and verbally incoherent in his efforts to reach the priest. The priest continued in his detached and somewhat calculating manner until finally he became aware of what it was doing to the man who was reaching for some kind of response. He stood up, turned to the group, and said, "I don't give a damn what the rest of you think." Then he went over to the man, embraced him, and wept. "I know what you are doing," he said. "No one has ever cared this much about me, to put himself in this kind of position." The group's response was an effusive but real demonstration of love. Embracing each other—beyond sex, beyond fear, beyond aggression—they were a vivid example of the intimacy our culture craves but so deeply fears.

The tension between the imposed ideal which discourages emotional expression—"Men don't cry"—and the inner self-image that saw the need for full expression of feeling had increased to the point where one had to "give." It was the false self-ideal that weakened first. How frequently we want to smell clean and look beautiful, thinking that this is sufficient for human dignity. So many of us who don't know who we are, are "friendly" with anyone who will keep us from finding out.

Blind Servant or Perceptive Master

If values imposed in childhood are incompatible with a person's self-ideal, or if the environment impedes their realization, he is often defensive. For instance, if the operative ideal is the fear of being caught and this alone prevents me from stealing, eventually the situation may arise where the fear is removed and I react against society. On the other hand, if the self-ideal includes the value of personal property, then the legal sanctions against thievery will not be a threat. Unfortunately, what the thief too frequently doesn't understand is that in exchange for material possessions he gives up his personal honesty.

When a person's activity is at odds with his self-image, there are two ways to reduce the discord. One is simply to change the behavior, and the other is to modify the image. The latter is the most effective therapy. I have met many people, for example, who recognize homosexual tendencies in themselves, or have indulged in homosexual behavior on occasion, and who, therefore, judge themselves to be homosexuals. As long as they persisted in this self-image, it was impossible for them to modify their behavior. When they could admit that having impulses toward members of their own sex did not make them irreversibly the stereotyped "homosexual" which they feared so deeply, then they could change their behavior.

The same sort of malady is seen in schizophrenic patients who judge themselves to be Jesus Christ, Napoleon Bonaparte or Teddy Roosevelt. Their behavior is compatible with their judgment and thus gives them the comfort of inner consistency, but puts them at odds with the larger society of men whose judgment differs radically.

We need to learn to recognize the basic consistency of the schizophrenic, the delinquent, and the homosexual. Rather than focus on the deviation or abnormality of their behavior, we might better try to find how this behavior makes some sense to them in facing their world. It may be ineffective behavior, and there may be incorrect perceptions of themselves or others. But if we recognize that *basically,* though not completely, a person aims for consistency in behaving according to his self-image and self-ideal, we are in a better position to discover what these are and how they might be changed. We must not be overeager, however, to invite others to reach for a laudable self-ideal, for this may add inconsistency to maladjustment. The behavior of a person who has a poor self-ideal and acts according to it may be maladaptive but at least it is consistent. If we ask him to act according to an ideal he really has not made his own, he may retain maladaptive behavior, being inconsistent both with his own self-image and the imposed self-ideal. His last state may be worse than the first, because now he is not only maladaptive, but also inconsistent. We tell the thief that it is wrong to steal, which he already knows, rather than convince him that he is not a thief. When we accomplish the latter, he may modify his behavior—not to please society, not to prove himself to us at the cost of inner inconsistency, but because those activities would no longer be compatible with his self-image.

Awareness and Behavior

In describing the relationship between behavior and the actual personality which it reveals, we can identify two fundamental sources of maladjustment. At the very basis of behavior is the person's self-knowledge, composed of self-image and self-ideal. Some people, of course, are much more explicit and much more accurate than others in what they know about themselves and what they do not know. But though everyone is more or less aware of who he is and what he is to become, there is a lot of room for blind spots and areas of ignorance. And it is precisely here that maladaptive behavior can sink roots.

The second source of maladaptive behavior lies in the inconsistency between awareness and behavior, a purposely chosen distortion of perception. For instance, the man who treats women exclusively on the level of physical gratification is closing his eyes to their higher personal values. Though he may be quite aware of the inconsistency of his behavior with the higher values that he holds, in this situation he chooses to ignore these values. Such maladaptive behavior has its own inner corrective, since the person is aware not only of the behavior itself but of the inconsistency involved in it. This awareness of inner disharmony eventually should encourage change. Personal integration aims at consistency and harmony. Unless the person goes to the point of shutting his eyes to the value of consistency itself, there is hope for change in any behavior.

It is my conviction that most maladaptive behavior is rooted in the first source—in an unconscious blindness of the person, in the covert dishonesty of a distorted self-image and self-ideal. Successful interaction with others, it seems to me, must make this assumption. Our relations with others should aim not so much at correcting inconsistencies in behavior as in increasing insight into self-image and self-ideal. Enduring changes in behavior follow from the expansion of awareness which we are led to in our relations with others.

People who tour a mental hospital are often amazed at how "normal" the patients seem. Perhaps when a patient is finally accepted as insane by those around him, he need no longer prove it, and he need not demonstrate the behavior that sent him there in the first place. By the same token, it is easier to control delinquent children in a detention home than outside. While authorities attribute this to the number of guards, they admit that they are outnumbered when faced by youthful ingenuity. In the delinquent home, where the youth is with peers who accept him in his own self-image as delinquent, he need not emphasize this fact by his behavior. Outside an environment that supports his self-image, an individual tends to become defensive about it. Uncertain of his self-image, he tends to assert it. The delinquent isn't quite sure that his self-image is accurate and reasserts it through delinquency. The psychotic is not quite sure he wants to be insane, for if he were convinced that the world is crazy and not he, he could feel comfortable among those that society judges sane.

Uncertainty of self-ideal causes problems also. In this situation we are easily threatened, tending to criticize those who disagree with our self-ideal, because we construe the disagreement as an attack. Parents who are uncertain of their own values are threatened by their children. As a result they make excessive demands that the children adhere to their dictates. If they were confident of their values and the way they have lived them, they still might become disappointed when their children do not adopt them, but they could allow them the freedom to choose their own. For if the parents' values are indeed worthwhile, they will not need to be imposed. Children may become what their parents *are*, not what they say, often to the consternation of the parents. Children quickly discern whether the parent *is* what he *says*, and if the discrepancy is great, they will very likely reject both.

Children Learn Who They Are from What We Are

The damage parents inadvertently inflict on children through their own dishonesty was demonstrated forcefully to me recently. In a group session, one seventeen-year-old girl named Chris was irritating the others in the group by her apparent disinterest. She was obviously masking a reluctance to open up to the group. Finally she told them that she had recently had an abortion and had come to see me because of the depression that followed the abortion. This statement was a surprise to me. Before the group session, I had seen Chris individually a few times, but neither she nor her parents had mentioned the abortion. Her parents had referred her to me because of her rebellious behavior at home and in school. They complained that she did not confide in them, could not be trusted, and was sneaky. Chris, in turn, accused her parents of being inconsistent, untrustworthy, and of punishing her unduly for little things. The boy friend involved was a minor who had, of course, promised to love, honor, obey, marry and spend eternity with Chris if she happened to become pregnant. When she did become pregnant, however, his attitudes changed. He promised to pay for the abortion, telling Chris he would deny paternity if she refused to have the abortion, but that she had to arrange the details. Though Chris had planned for them to marry when they reached eighteen (the legal age of the state), the boy friend now backed out. Chris, frightened that her parents would reject her, did not go to them for help. "They would just think I'm an old slut, a whore; they're close enough to thinking it now." So the secret was locked inside Chris; and even when she shared it with a few girl friends, this did not alleviate the guilt, the anxiety, and the fear of being punished.

When she had talked of suicide at home, her parents were upset and came to my office. They felt guilty and asked how they could have caused their daughter to be so different. Characteristically, they laid the blame on "the crowd she hangs around with." After some time listening to them evade their own responsibility, I finally asked them if they really wanted to find out what was at the root of their daughter's behavior. (As far as I know, they still do not know about the abortion.) When I asked them to look into their own lives for the dishonesty between them which might explain the dishonesty in Chris, the father protested vehemently. There was no dishonesty in their marriage, he told me. It was a "beautiful marriage and there's nothing wrong with it."

At this point his wife began to cry. "Why don't you tell him the truth?" she pleaded.

He came back forcefully, "I told you not to mention that."

A verbal struggle between the two ensued in my office, the one angry because he had been exposed, and the other crying for help. In a short time they both turned against me, claiming that they had not come to my office to talk about themselves, that I had not told them about their girl, and that it was their right to know what Chris was telling me in the office. This climate of dishonesty between the parents who repeatedly entrenched themselves in their mutual alienation was wrecking their daughter. And her own fear of her parents was nothing but a facade to avoid her responsibility for the situation she was trapped in. She was caught, angry at life—and at the dishonesty of her parents and herself—and afraid of exposing these feelings to the group for fear they would not understand but reject her. The values the parents had unwittingly transmitted were directly opposed to the values they talked about. Though tragic, the situation was not surprising. The truth of the person is seldom adequately concealed and often seeps through the most carefully chosen words.

When a person's self-image is compatible with his ideal of what he ought to be, his behavior will enhance the judgment. When he knows where he is and where he wants to go, what he does will confirm his confidence. He will be comfortable with himself and relatively secure of where he is going. Even when people disagree with him, he will not be preoccupied with defending himself, but will follow the convictions he has built up and so confirm and sustain the compatibility of image and ideal.

PRESERVING THE TOTAL PERSONALITY

The values which are expressed in behavior must reflect the whole person if they are to lead toward maturity. Unfortunately, many theorists have focused on special aspects of behavior to the exclusion of the whole. Freud, perhaps the most famous of these, assumed that all needs were ultimately biological and that the primary expression of needs is found in sexuality. Freud was aware of needs on all levels of personality (within the humanist framework) but he minimized the intellectual aspect by insisting on the fulfillment of sexual needs. While most psychotherapists will agree that they seldom see a patient without a sexual problem, I would add that I have seldom seen a person whose sexual problem was not a manifestation of a more deeply rooted problem, namely a disruption in the basic love relationship. Freud was so impressed by the long over-looked importance of sexuality and so struck by the universality of sexual problems that his discovery led him to take an exaggerated position. Assuming that sex was the basic driving force of man and his most critical personality function, he claimed that all problems were at root *nothing but* sexual problems. Freud's true genius, however, lay in the unearthing of unconscious motives. But when this startling revelation was combined with his talk about sex in a Victorian era, his psychotherapeutic revolution was blown up all out of proportion.

The era of tranquilizers has brought another limited picture of man. When tranquilizers were introduced several years ago, it was hoped that they would clear up mental illness, but this hope has not been realized. Before the age of tranquilizers, 50 percent of hospital beds in the United States were occupied by mentally ill patients, and this figure has remained relatively unchanged. Before tranquilizers, the average length of hospitalization for the mentally ill patient was about twenty years, and this figure also remains approximately the same. Tranquilizers do alleviate *symptoms* of mentally ill patients so that less discomfort is found and less cruel restraints are necessary on the hospital ward. They have in fact replaced the strait-jacket. But the enthusiasm of physicians over the discovery of tranquilizers was based on the erroneous assumption that man's mental and emotional problems were *nothing but* the product of physiological impairment. The term mental "illness" is, in fact, a grand myth in that most mental illnesses arise from incorrect judgments rather than the breakdown of the physical system. Tranquilizers mask the symptoms but do little to change the course of the disease. As long as the cause of mental or emotional disturbance, i.e., improper judgments, is untouched, the disturbance will continue no matter how long the patient is sedated.

Still another limited picture of man came in the wake on intelligence testing tended to blur other aspects of in education, it was assumed that by determining the basic intelligence of a student, all sorts of academic, social, and personal problems could be solved. This focus on intelligence testing tended to blur other aspects of personality, especially the emotional and biological functions.

Although physiological and emotional functions need to be harmonized with intellectual and critical functions, they are not to be equated with them. As the personality grows, intelligence operates more independently, but some link to emotional and physical factors will always remain. The person involved in an "emotional argument" is one whose conclusions are more determined by the emotions of the situation than the reasonable truth of the matter. A person whose emotions and intelligence are well integrated can use his emotional strength to aid reasonable courses of action. But physical and emotional factors must be met before reasonable choices can be made. The student who is interested in college for monetary reasons alone will probably function less adequately than the student who is fascinated by the experiences opened to him in new vistas of knowledge. The statement of one eighteen-year-old is sadly typical: "I just don't believe any more that I have to go to college to make a better living. My family is very wealthy and I am going to be taken care of financially quite well, no matter what I do. I'm sick and tired of the whole mess. I just wish, once in my career, someone had told me I ought to go to school to learn. This is why I want to go to school, and someday I will go. But my dropping out of high school is the only way I know to tell my parents that they are wrong in asking me to go to college so I can earn more money when I get out. I know it's going to shake them up a bit but I hope they will realize that even though money may be their god, it is not mine. I will return to school even if they don't realize this, but I can't ignore the opportunity to help them with this problem."

My Behavior Is Me

Behavior is not only a part of man; in a sense it *is* man. As the people around us reject our behavior, they reject us. The importance of interpersonal relations to behavior cannot be overemphasized. This point has come back to me repeatedly, as it did in the case of sixteen-year-old Linda.

When Linda first came to me, she was already a habitual drug user and sexually promiscuous. Before long she ran away from home but kept in contact with me because she continued to trust me—much to the chagrin of her parents who at one point seemed to be attempting to force me to break her confidence. She also maintained contact with a therapy group of girls to whom she had confided. After several long-distance conversations with her group, Linda was convinced to come back but to a foster home since she refused to return to her parents. "My parents," she said, "don't accept me. They don't love me." The parents insisted, on the other hand, that they did love and accept her. At one session with both the parents and Linda, I asked them outright, "What would you rather have your daughter doing, out prostituting on the streets feeling that she was being true to herself, or entering a convent feeling that it was what you wanted her to do?" The mother was quick to respond, "I would never permit my daughter to be a prostitute. I would rather see her dead."

The girl walked out of the office and refused to see her parents for several weeks. The mother missed the point that by her attitude she was, in fact, rejecting her child because Linda's values were at variance with her own. Linda, however, did not miss the point, and did not return home until the mother could accept her as a person in spite of her immoral behavior. Fortunately, with help, the parents later were able to discover how their own fears were blocking perception of the underlying causes of their child's behavior. Then they realized that until she could be accepted with her maladaptive behavior, as she was, Linda would not have the freedom to change. As long as her parents kept insisting on moral behavior on their terms, the child continued to react against those values. Further therapy has helped her overcome many of the obstacles to her growth.

Attack: Subtle Permission

We tend to criticize in others what we fear in ourselves. When we condemn others for their sins, we may really fear our own weakness. Perhaps we are secretly participating in the same sins, or wish we could, or fear we might. We persecute others to keep them from discovering the forces that lurk inside us. In attacking their failures, we can vicariously overcome fear of the same failure in ourselves.

One particularly sad case dramatizes the point. Several years ago a man came to my office to have his wife "repaired." Complaining of her immaturity and her inefficiency as wife and mother, he asked me what I could do with her. "I'm an engineer," he explained, "and when something goes wrong, I go to someone who can fix it. My wife has been acting strangely. I went to four medical specialists, and all of them concurred that there is nothing physically wrong with her. So I decided to bring her to you. Fix her. I'll pay whatever it costs." I invited him to remain, but he refused, insisting that the difficulty lay completely with his wife.

In talking with his wife, I discovered a confused, childish, and maladjusted woman, who kept complaining that her husband only treated her as a thing. It was clear that in his engineer's mode of dealing with the world, she was simply another piece of machinery. Improvement being impossible without his cooperation, he soon withdrew her from therapy, and they were divorced shortly thereafter. She became a chronic alcoholic and died three years later of cirrhosis of the liver, a forsaken woman, living off welfare on skid-row.

The husband remarried and, I believe, is having similar difficulties with his new wife. The children show pitiful signs of their father's severe dishonesty and lack of love. His six-year-old son is already suffering from ulcers. His eldest daughter, a bright student, went into medical school but developed so severe a neurosis that she was forced to discontinue her studies. She remains unmarried and seriously maladjusted. Of his three children, only one is doing well, after extensive treatment; he is married, has two children and is holding down a good teaching job. But the vicious chain of damage has hardly ended, and probably will not until the father can look into himself with a sincere desire to change, instead of projecting his fears of self-worthlessness onto those around him.

When others accept us, we can consider ourselves as worthwhile and begin to develop our potentialities. We shape our own images by this acceptance, forming values as we communicate with others in our lives. When others consider us worthwhile, our image forms accordingly and behavior will manifest this self-image.

The values that shape our lives are not formed in isolation but are greatly affected by the "significant others" in our lives. Once I can consider myself worthwhile, through acceptance by another, I can regard myself as worthy enough to share with others.

COMMUNICATION AS TOTAL SHARING

Sharing knowledge is the highest form of human behavior. The youngest children eagerly trade information with each other. A child who likes a playmate will tell him a secret. Even adults who constantly look for juicy bits of gossip to share with someone are trying to achieve some basis for a human relationship. Intellectual sharing among people is actually so important that a relationship based merely on communicating neutral information is somewhat satisfying. How much more meaningful is an intimate relationship in which deep personal knowledge is shared. An adequate person wants to do more than pick the brains of his professor, and the adequate professor wants to do more than transmit knowledge to his students.

Intimacy: Possibility or Myth

Wouldn't it be wonderful if one human being could totally share himself with another! Imagine a situation in which they could communicate intimately, not only on an intellective level, but also on an emotional level; a sharing not only of ideas, but also an intimate sharing of feelings and attitudes. Add to this a physiological sharing where each could encompass the other intimately and physically. And imagine this intimate total communication aimed toward a goal beyond both of them, an extension of themselves, a creation beyond themselves in which each was participating and enriching the other's personality at one and the same time. Imagine all these things and you have ideal love, the creative result of total communication and sharing of one human being with another.

A communication that involves the total personality of one human being interacting with the total personality of another human being, creating a continuation of both of them, an act in which they both participate, is the highest form of human love. And the highest expression of the commitment of that kind of human love can be through sexual intercourse. What a tragedy that sexuality has been so poorly understood and so often used as less than a communication of the total person. How unfortunate that the sexual revolution of the past few years has deteriorated into a physiological and emotional outburst that ignores the intellective and creative aspects of the human personality. How unfortunate that sexual activity, potentially the most human love act, is often so unhealthy because it is so misunderstood. Partners, each totally giving himself, each totally receptive to the other in the creation of a new life—two human beings can come no closer to perfect love than this mutual sharing, this completing of each other's nature.

Love between two human beings requires a judgment of value. When I experience love for someone, I affirm his worth and mine also. I judge that he is worthwhile, totally and completely, that I am worth this other person, and that together we are good enough to produce another person like us and to care for him. It is the expression of this intellective affirmation of communication and sharing that is the highest aspect of sexual intercourse—not the physiological release of tension. But the fact that such a value judgment is being expressed through the physical act of sexual intercourse will increase the physiological gratification.

To engage in sexual intercourse without this judgmental appreciation is a dehumanizing thing. In a very important sense, sex is a "technique" for gaining intimacy, not a substitute for it. To take the ultimate that can occur in human activity, the highest form of love, and to abuse it for the sake of physical gratification, is detrimental to one's own person as well as to the person of another.

Sexuality: Sharing or Control

Sexual release can occur on a physiological basis, by-passing intellective judgments, and even by-passing emotional involvement. Prostitution and masturbation are common examples. The prostitute does not want to know the name of her client, since if she were to become emotionally involved with him she would no longer have him as a customer. The natural repulsiveness that many people feel towards prostitution is the realization that the prostitute is abusing and dehumanizing herself. Most people are repulsed when a fine intricate machine is abused—how much more abhorrent to see a human being abused, even if it is self-abuse. This is so apparent that a *truly* mature man could not function sexually with a prostitute. The idea of using another human being purely and simply for physical gratification without an affirmation of the value of that person would be abhorrent to him. Physiology subserves the value judgment so that he literally could not maintain a penile erection. To enjoy relations with a prostitute the male must forget about her *as a person,* using her solely as an object of physical gratification rather than as a human being in order to go through with the act. The world's oldest profession flourishes because of men's immaturity, not because of the manliness of the immature, as the defenders of prostitution might claim.

In a college fraternity initiation rite a few years ago,

several men were to engage in sexual intercourse with the same woman. One of the pledges awaited his turn. When the moment arrived, he hopped into bed only to find his sister lying there. The boy became physically ill and eventually became mentally deranged. The confrontation with the fact that others had dehumanized a human being he loved was more than he could cope with.

Masturbation, although a normal outlet in today's culture and society, is also an immature expression of sexuality. It is a gratification or a release of tension that is normally not harmful, but not fulfilling either, and it does not enhance personality growth. There has been so much mystery and misinformation about masturbation that it is important to insist that it should not be considered unnatural but merely immature. Masturbation is a normal part of the growth process. It is abnormal only if it continues into adulthood and replaces adequate sexual involvement in a true love relationship. For an immature adolescent to masturbate is normal, but a married person who masturbates may be doing so because something is wrong in his love relationship with his mate.

Sexuality is such a critical human function that many people, including Freud, assumed that it was *the* critical human function. Freud (and others) failed to go beyond sexuality to find its basis—the human relationship. In his focus on sex, to the exclusion of the more basic driving forces in the person, Freud may have done some damage to cultural and social growth.

The ability to function sexually is not a valid criterion of human maturity. Any animal can do as much, and most at a considerably earlier age. Though sexual functioning is something we share generically with animals, human maturity is not attained so effortlessly or assuredly. Indulging in sexual play at fifteen or seventeen does not make a teenager a man or a woman. The adolescent who engages in sexual intercourse at a teenage level without meeting the human responsibility of such activity is at best demonstrating his immaturity, and at worst creating serious personality damage that goes far beyond himself.

If sexual intercourse is to be engaged in at a level that commits one's total personality and serves the integration with another personality, several things are demanded. First the person must value himself as worthwhile, as having something worth giving to another person. The other person must prize himself in the same manner. Both partners must be convinced that what they have is worth reproducing, either in having their own children or in raising adopted children.

In our culture, sexual intercourse outside of marriage is not a totally human act, no matter what rationalizations or defenses are used to support it. Sexuality can be totally given and shared with no real loss of oneself. To engage in sexual activity without the fulfillment of both personalities by extending the relationship into a permanent love "commitment" is an insult to human dignity. Such fulfillment demands social restrictions, limitations, and responsibilities. Sex outside of committed marriage erects a barrier to the full expression of the person. The contradiction implied in the expression of total sharing without an explicit commitment to the future will inevitably cause frustration.

Sexual intercourse is not specifically an inborn physiological need. A man can survive quite well without fulfilling it on a physical level. Love can be expressed emotionally and intellectually even though no physiological expression takes place. Sex as a subsystem separate from love would be similar to the hunger drive in man. But when sex is considered as part of love, one can block the physiological sexual urge and still be a whole person. A man who does not engage in sexual activity when his wife is ill is not considered less a man. On the contrary, the man who would go to a prostitute because his wife is sick would indeed be considered immature. Sex should subserve love rather than be independent of it. Love demands either mature sexuality or its suppression for the sake of a goal that transcends normal everyday human functioning. Love is primarily an intellective phenomenon, an affirmation of value. When sex is engaged in apart from this affirmation of value, it is a deteriorating force in human personality.

Marriage: Payment or Intimacy

In several years of practice, I have seen much human disharmony and disturbance. In very few cases did a couple, while admitting some sexual difficulties with each other, honestly judge that their difficulties were more basic. One couple, in particular, stands out—people who wanted more than sexual adequacy, who wanted sharing and communication on all levels, and who recognized that successful physical cohabitation would not solve their problems though they knew that a solution to their problems would eventuate in exciting physical cohabitation.

It was only a matter of a few short sessions before this

couple understood the necessity of sharing on all levels and their need to choose and affirm each other on all levels. To watch the need for intimacy transcend any particular level of functioning in the therapeutic progress of these two people was beautiful to witness. As they grew, they were able to open up to each other honestly, to confront each other and say *with increased meaning,* "I love you." They could talk without fear, expressing negative feelings without danger of rejection and then positive feelings without embarrassment. Their attachment increased as they became open and kindly critical of each other; love and trust developed and new-found freedom emerged.

I watched the authenticity of these two people as the façade dropped and honesty emerged. I saw them assist each other, not because they needed each other, but because they chose each other. I could follow this development to its end in the fulfillment and completion of their personalities. I could observe the exposure of one personality to another, the ripping away of masks. The inevitable growth that occurred in their encounter confirmed my conviction of the possibility of deep and intimate love. When these two people totally exposed themselves to each other by choice, not by coercion, fear dissipated and guilt diminished. Intimacy without fear displaced apprehensive closeness.

Any of us can have a new experience of self and of another if we are willing to work for it. Total interpersonal involvement and total interpersonal exposure without inhibition, guilt, or fear must occur on every level, physical, emotional, intellectual, and spiritual. People can learn to love, deeply and meaningfully. Our sexual, emotional, and intellectual difficulties can decrease as love grows, and when we meet friends, neighbors, and associates, this healthy attitude will spread.

Is perfect love humanly possible? The increased ability to love with total exposure of person to person on every level again raises that question. We have seen how every organism tries to incorporate its environment and how through knowledge this is achieved intellectively by men. We have seen also how knowledge shared is not diminished and how in the fullest human expression of love in sexual intercourse maximum sharing and union on all levels of personality occur with no loss of self.

What a person offers in a love relationship is himself in his totality. What he receives is another self in its totality. But each of these gifts is also a personality in the process of growth and, to some extent, incomplete. It is the mutual possession and sharing of each other that is the new unity, the "we." Yet, each, in giving himself, wants the completion of the other. In this total sharing and manifestation of himself, the lover realizes that there are elements of himself that are limited, that are less than they might be.

To be perfect, love must accomplish the complete unity of both persons. But because there are elements of the underdeveloped and the corrupt in each partner, love looks beyond the present to the union of two perfect selves and realizes that it is always in process and not complete. The lover wants to share his whole being and wants to take into himself the being of the beloved. But as love heightens his self-awareness he sees also his depravity, his negative self-love, his weakness, his indolence. He asks himself whether he is not infecting his beloved with his depravity. And the more he loves, the more he fears poisoning the beloved with what is corrupt in himself. He desires to share and reveal all he is, but part of what he is may, he feels, harm the one he loves.

In this dialetic of human love we see the highest of human activities. Being imperfect, we are then led to consider the possibility of the perfect love promised by human love when it functions at its highest level. Saint John clearly expresses it for us in his first letter. "God is love, and anyone who lives in love, lives in God and God lives in him" (1 John 4:16).

4

Love: The Abandonment of Power

WE HAVE been tracing man's search for an honest, loving relationship to his fellow-man. To know who I am, I must reach out to someone else for help. But because I fear his response, I am inclined to reveal myself only partially. I pick and choose what I know of myself in order to control the reflection that comes back; I screen questions in order to insure answers. I give way to small dishonesties and begin to build up a façade. I avoid the tensions that could lead to growth and let the values I fear losing remain unexamined. The evidence of hiding, holding back, lashing out destructively, and running in fear is overwhelming and eventually I am led to ask whether love is possible at all. Love begins to look like a mirage on the horizon, perhaps a possibility for other men but only an unattainable ideal for me. If I am doomed to fail, does it really matter how I choose to behave? In this chapter we will set down two alternative modes of living which are presented to man in the form of basic options: the option for love and the option for power.

THE BASIC OPTIONS

Only rarely do we find in human beings an unequivocal dedication to either power or love. Most of us vacillate between these two fundamental modes of living without ever committing ourselves wholeheartedly to either one. Nevertheless, by isolating the characteristics of each mode, we can present ourselves with a standard for examining the general orientation of our life-choices.

Our technological and consumer-oriented society can serve as an image of the *power* mode of living. Not only do we seek by ever more sophisticated techniques to gain mastery over our external environment, but we extend this quest for control into our relationships with other men. Not only do we "take" our pleasures, our entertainment, and our cures, but we tend to value other men in terms of what they can "give" us.

But there is an alternate mode of living, the mode of *love*. While power captures and consumes, love gently embraces and then sets free. Even if we find ourselves unable to choose the form of love consistently, we cherish the hope that it is possible at least some of the time with some persons. We may remain in the power pattern of living, but never abandon the hope that it is possible for us to let go of power and open our arms in love.

Henri J. M. Nouwen sets out the two alternatives succinctly:

Our plan is first to describe carefully and understand the two main forms of existing, the form of power and the form of love, or, in other words, the taking form and the forgiving form, and secondly to examine how these forms are related to destruction and to creation. Only then are we ready to ask the crucial question: Is love a utopian dream or a possibility within our reach? [1]

But it is not enough to expose the possibility of love in general; it must be seen as possible *for me*. Moreover, it must be something that I find desirable and am willing to work for. Perhaps we might be better persuaded to let go of power if we could see where it leads us.

We frequently entertain the illusion that if we let go of the control we exercise over our life and the lives of others, somehow our life will be drained of all its joys and pleasures. Actually, the reverse is true. Our sensitivities are not deadened but opened up to new levels of experience once they have been charged with meaning and purpose. In the power mode, desirability is measured by how often sensation occurs and how intense it is, while in loving, what is desirable depends on the meaning of the object and our commitment to it.

Marriage is the ideal situation for experiencing the depth of meaning that the love mode can reveal. Two people, committed to one another in marriage and willing to suffer the pain and setbacks of abandoning their controls over one another can reap the rewards of a forgiving and loving relationship. The destructiveness that results when man and wife cohabitate in the power mode, resorting to power tactics and strict *quid pro quo* contracts, eventually reaches the point of irreversibility and inevitably the loving mode loses its appeal and meaning.

The Paradox of Love

The paradox of the loving mode is that it is simple but difficult. Letting go of one's power is a matter of simple choice, but an extremely painful one when it is shrouded by the fear of losing one's value in the process. For to give up the power mode of life is truly an abandonment of the security of controlling other people, of the shelter for the vulnerability of the secrets of our hearts. The way of power is secured at the expense of maintaining adequate defenses, while the way of love demonstrates a willingness to be defenseless. In our power-hungry society it is not at all surprising that the disproportionate amount of time individuals spend on self-defense of personality is accurately reflected in our national budget where defense costs rise higher and higher each year.

ɩ To the loving person, other men are seen as valuable in themselves, not as usable objects. Love does not capture, use, or destroy, but invites freedom and growth. But in the stance of power, it is the fear of my own lack of value that must be protected. Afraid that I am worth nothing, I dare not expose too much of myself, for any opening in my armor is an opportunity for others to take advantage of that total vulnerability. Likewise, any new crisis or tension is seen as a *threat* to my position as victor in the control of my life. It is only when power is abandoned that such tension can be seen as a *challenge* to growth, as the pains of birth rather than a battle ground from which I must, at all costs, emerge the victor.

How I value myself depends on what I have learned

about myself from others, and particularly from my parents. If the financial struggles of the family are allowed to rule the relationship between parents and child, there is a subtle communication of personal worth as something which can be labeled with a price tag. Paul, a twenty-year-old of whom I am quite fond, told me how upset his parents became when he told them he was thinking about buying a motorcycle. "We have wasted twenty years of our lives on you," was their comment. This young man is a truly good person who is struggling to live honestly and discover himself. What can he learn about his own value from parents who feel they have wasted their lives on him because they are no longer able to control him? My anger often reaches extremes at parents who teach their children that they are worth so little; but then a moment's reflection tells me that they were probably taught the same thing by their parents. The Christian tradition symbolizes this reality in "original sin": that the dishonesties of one generation are transmitted unconsciously to the next.

In contrast is Fred, a young man who expressed interest to me in going on a marathon session. In the interview prior to the session, I told him that I felt he really did not *need* to participate in group therapy. In fact, I predicted that if he chose to come, it would be painful for him to witness the damage that dishonesty had wrought. "I still would like to go," Fred insisted, "because I want to get closer to people." As it turned out, it took him only a few minutes to open up to the group and tell them of the love he had experienced in

his childhood. His life had not been completely un-
sullied, but on the occasions when he had failed to love,
there was someone who cared in his life, someone to
whom he could always turn. It has been my experience
that the rare persons who have had a life so devoid of
hiding have been able to speak of their parents as people
who loved one another and were not afraid to show it.

It is my judgment of another's value that makes it
possible for me to love him. That his worth exists
whether at first I am aware of it or not does not mean
that I am able to love everyone to the same degree. Very
often, for example, my decision to work with a person
goes contrary to the dislike I may feel toward him; it is
only because of an awareness of a deeper value that I
can make such a commitment. It usually happens that
as he is able to see his own worth more clearly, he also
becomes much more likeable to me. But the judgment
of an individual's value as the basis for love must be
independent of the immediate emotions he stirs up. I
can make a commitment to his value and still help him
face my feelings as well as his own. I can hardly pretend
to love everyone equally. It would be a counterfeit sort
of love that always demanded emotion and feeling for
its base. Values and judgments of worth may endure,
while feelings and emotions change frequently.

FEELINGS AND CHOICE

These two styles of life, power and love, have widely
divergent effects on the way we perceive other men and

respond to them. In the power mode we perceive others as *objects* to be controlled; in the loving mode we value them as *persons* with whom we can share ourselves. We need to look more carefully at the effects of our perceptions on our emotions, in order that we may act in accordance with our chosen mode of living. In every encounter with another person, there are three basic possibilities for relating to him, each with its own emotional component. The desire to move towards him generates the emotion of *affection;* the desire to remove him from our presence leads to *anger;* and the desire to move away is supported by the emotion of *fear.* These three emotional states with which people relate to one another—affection, anger, and fear—are fundamental.

Fortunately, between the emotion and its corresponding action, a whole range of choices is available to us. In addition we have the use of memory and imagination to assist us in formulating our choices. Our memory allows us to associate present perceptions with past ones so we may deal with new situations in terms of habits reinforced over a period of time. Care must be exercised, however, not to let habitual responses take the place of sound judgment. This is the root of prejudice. In my own case, for example, having been raised in an environment that fostered prejudice toward blacks, I was not able to free myself of it until some Negroes were willing to help me deal with my stereotypes and my fears. Only then could I see individual blacks in their uniqueness rather than as instances of certain images I had—images based on a few fragmented experiences explained by misunderstandings I had learned.

Imagining the Possibilities

Man also can imagine. He can construct possible situations to serve as a link between the raw, habitual emotions and his future choices for action. He can imagine different actions and their consequences, and can evaluate them. Often, however, imagination is constricted because certain choices have been learned as threatening and fear thus narrows down the vision of imagination. For instance, a person may become frightened if he imagines himself killing another person or sexually abusing someone he loves, so strong is the association between these fantasies and the choices they suggest. And yet imagination leaves us free to direct our actions according to judgment rather than by habit. Attraction need not necessarily lead to control; anger need not lead to violence; and fear need not lead to escape. We are subject to emotions but we need not be the victims of them, so long as we can choose to base our actions on value-judgments rather than on impulses.

The misunderstanding of emotions generally occurs when we refuse to recognize their presence. It is often very comfortable to avoid our feelings, but it is much more mature to deal effectively with them. A person who feels sexual attraction to another *can* admit these feelings to himself and feel free to express them to the other person without choosing to engage in immature or harmful behavior. A person who is angry with another man may likewise admit his feelings and express them without resorting to a violent act which may remove the possibility of discovering the source of that anger. Finally, one may be afraid of another person, admit his fear and choose to face the threatening situation rather than run from it.

Dishonesty enters when we become ashamed of ourselves for being the sort of person who experiences inappropriate sentiments within himself. A mother may be angry at her child and imagine smashing its head against the wall; a father may be sexually attracted to his daughter and have fantasies of becoming physically involved with her. But because mothers should not kill their own children and fathers should not commit incest, even the fact that such a fantasy occurs to them is enough to terrify them into denying their own feelings. Such threatening fantasies then subtly convince them that they are inwardly very wicked people who must hide their imagined activity from other men. It is only when we can meet our emotions head-on that we are capable of responsible and free choices.

Emotions: Guideposts or Obstacles

The manner in which a person deals with his emotions, as we might expect, differs in the power and loving modes of living. In the way of power, *attraction* is a function of the usefulness of the other person for our own needs. Sexual attraction is a function of the pleasure derived from sexual release or the security experienced in having someone near, irrespective of the growth of either person. In its extreme, such abuse of persons leads to prostitution or rape. But more commonly, much of what passes for legal and accepted sexuality suffers under the same gross misuse of persons. The mutual masturbation of teenage couples is really no different from the sexual activity of the married who betray a power mentality in the capturing, seducing, controlling, and manipulating quest for sexual fulfillment. Sexuality that depends only on the variety of positions, the frequency of intercourse, and the insistence on mutual orgasm all betray the power mode of sexual attraction. Such a relation is doomed to inevitable apathy and callousness towards the possibility of a true and intimate love willing to endure sacrifice for the sake of growth. It is accompanied by the haunting terror of rejection when one becomes useless to his mate, when pleasure wanes, and when the focus of attraction shifts to another party.

Suppressing or Expressing Anger

In the power mode, *anger* is expressed in the desire to destroy. Here we generally attempt to control or enslave the object of our anger. When we cannot succeed in this effort, our only alternative is to escape the situation rather than risk being controlled by the other person. In the loving mode, on the other hand, anger is recognized as anger and expressed as concern. First we make the effort to understand the cause of the anger. If we find it in ourselves, we must try to change; or, if it is in the other, we may invite him, out of true concern, to change himself. Love transforms anger into care. In the loving person anger always conveys the hope that the immature behavior generating the anger will be corrected. If people were incapable of changing, anger would be totally inappropriate, a useless passion. But when anger is motivated by true concern, it need lose none of its strength and sensitivity.

I recall vividly one such case in a marathon session. A young man who was unable to break through his inhibitions seemed to be going around in circles. Fatigue had begun to overtake the group and several of them spontaneously began to pull away from him, giving him up to his own freely chosen isolation. Suddenly, one member of the group, a man about twenty-seven, ran over to the young man, literally picked him up by the collar and pinned him against the wall, screaming at him, "Can't you see that I really love you? Good God, what do I have to do, kill you to prove it?" This honest expression of anger finally made the young man realize that he was surrounded by people who really did care enough to share his own pains of growth with him. This was all he needed to let go of his defensive controls and break out of his isolation.

Finally, *fear* in the power mode of living creates in us the desire to run from a situation or person that we judge to be beyond our control. For, in the power mode, where control over the situation or person is the goal, our fear of losing such control must result in an effort to escape in one way or another. Often it leads us to strengthen our defenses or to adopt a variety of dodges to escape the threatening situation. In the loving mode, however, fear need not result in running. This is not to say that we will cease to become frightened or disarmed when we open our souls, for the fear of rejection always accompanies any total revelation of the self to another. It merely means that we can choose to disclose ourselves in spite of our fear, under the hope that with the growth of love, the fear will gradually be dissipated. The perfect love which drives out fear is the goal in every human relationship in the loving mode.

These three emotions we have been describing—affection, anger, and fear—are rarely discovered alone, but usually cloak themselves in one another's disguises. Everyone is familiar, for example, with the bully who covers his fear with anger, or conversely, with the shy person who retires behind his timidity because he fears the anger within him. Sexuality, while it may be the expression of affectionate emotions, may also blanket fear or anger. A man who is insecure with his masculinity may act out sexually to mask the fear. This is especially true if he is afraid of homosexual tendencies, in which case he may purposely seek heterosexual affairs to prove to himself that his fear is unfounded.

Much dishonesty results from the confusion of underlying emotions. When we are honest and loving, however, we can face our emotions for what they are and make appropriate choices in the face of what we discover about ourselves. When our choices are adequate, they become a means to effective growth. On the other hand, when we disguise our emotions or handle them dishonestly, we obstruct our own growth and make self-understanding an impossibility.

Fear Can Be Faced Honestly

Several cases may help to clarify what we have been saying. Daniel, a young man who took part in a recent marathon session, appeared, at first glance, to be quite honest, apparently showing no signs of aggressive or

sexual dishonesty. But as he continued to talk, it became clear that something was still missing in his revelation of himself. Daniel could not really let go with his
feelings, even though he didn't hide from the ones he
was able to expose. The session appeared to reach a
standstill. All I knew was that for some reason Daniel
was still enslaved by his own inhibitions, unfree to let
go of what was inside him.

I suggested that we enact symbolically where he
seemed to be. I asked him if he would be willing to be
handcuffed to me physically, since that seemed to express our confusion with one another. He became terrified, turned pale, and broke out in a cold sweat. His
whole body quivered and his hands became wet with
perspiration. He said he didn't know what it all meant,
or why he was becoming so frightened, but that he
wanted to find out. So the cuffs were locked on us and
the key given to the other therapist. We ended up spend-
ing about fifteen hours chained together, with all the
pain and discomfort this involved in eating, sleeping,
smoking, and the like.

Eventually, as a mutual dependency formed between
us, we began to explore areas in our lives that might be
the true cause for the chaining. We both became more
and more aware that the real chains were not the cold
steel cuffs around our wrists, but that somehow we were
controlling one another, manipulating one another, enslaving one another. It finally came out that Daniel, a
Jew, had been the victim of severe prejudice. Raised in
a Christian neighborhood, he had often been beaten up
and labeled kike and Christ-killer. He had never come
to understand such viciousness, and while he himself

could see that this was not a Christian characteristic, he could not understand how others could have abused him without ever knowing anything more about him than his religion. Others in the group, Christians of one denomination or another, responded by revealing the experiences they had had with Jews and the prejudices they had formed on the basis of those experiences.

Daniel discovered that he could get close to others without the fear of being misunderstood, that he could question others about their prejudices, and that he could reveal the feelings of hurt that had churned inside of him since childhood. In his courage and willingness to be chained to me, Daniel was able symbolically to relive lost feelings and release them. He experienced, as he expressed it later, a tremendous liberation from the fear he had been burdened with and chained to for so many years. No one could have faced his fear for him, but the presence of honest people who cared for him made it possible for him to face his own fear.

Often when we are confronted with a person who wants to face his unknown fears, we instinctively try to run from the situation because we become stirred up ourselves. When this happens, people whom we should care about are left captured by fear and may even be worse off for having reached out and been ignored. A nun came to see me about a year ago, feeling guilty and worthless because she had been masturbating. She was rather attractive but very lonely and quite naïve about her own sexuality. She felt isolated from those around her and feared revealing her own lack of understanding to them, all the while torturing herself because of her chronic problem. Finally the tension got so strong that she confided in a fellow sister about the sexual immaturity that was bothering her. But instead of helping her face the fear, the other nun became frightened herself and began to keep away. Eventually she requested a transfer, leaving the first nun only more isolated and hurt. Though the two women could have faced their fears together, the situation ended up worse than it had begun.

But Honesty Can Frighten Others

On one marathon session, Betty, a sexually promiscuous young woman who had been using drugs, was trying to be as open as she could with the group. As she told us where she was in her own growth, she revealed how impossible it seemed for her to be honest with her parents since they continually hid from her. I told her that her parents had expressed similar complaints to me about her. As a result of the session, Betty decided to try to be more open with her father, since she felt that would make him more likely to be honest with her. Once home, she took a pound of marijuana she had been keeping and disposed of it. Then she went to her father and told him that she had been hiding from him, relating how she had just disposed of the marijuana in an effort to better her life. He reacted in shock and merely replied, "I wish you hadn't told me that." He walked out of the room. Betty called me late that night, very disturbed by her father's reaction. I invited her to come over to the house, and my wife and I stayed up with her to talk about what had happened and tried to restore her courage in reaching out to people. If only

Betty's father had had the maturity to face his own fears instead of discarding them, he could have helped his daughter through a very difficult change in her life.

An honest person inevitably frightens dishonest people because he generates in them the fear of what they have not faced in themselves. In their fear they will either run, attack or reexamine themselves. The honest life carries with it no guarantees of security and comfort, and all too frequently ends at the hands of the violent who are too afraid to question their own lives.

From Fear and Anger to Love

When we have been paralyzed by fear for a long time, we begin to lose hope that we can overcome it at all. But if at least once we do succeed in doing so, hope returns and further effort to face our fears is possible. We are en-*couraged*. Sometimes this occurs when we "forget" to be afraid or when we act in the face of fear.

Joe was a twenty-one-year-old man whom I had been seeing off and on for over eight years in private therapy, with very little progress. Often our encounters with one another ended in uncommunicative silence. Ridden with scrupulosity, Joe would go from church to church to confess his sins and rid himself of his guilt feelings. Finally he enrolled in a group session. About two weeks before it was scheduled to begin, he called me up at four o'clock in the morning, threatening to commit suicide. In my judgment, his call was an immature use of power to get my attention. I was quite angry at him and told him so. "What are you doing, calling me up at this hour of the night? Look, you have an appointment for three o'clock this afternoon. I'll see you then. If you're going to kill yourself before then, I'm not powerful enough to keep you from it. I will mourn you, but I will go on living." Of course, I slept less comfortably the rest of the night, not knowing for sure whether I'd find him alive in my office in the afternoon or be informed of his death. I certainly do not recommend this as a general pattern for responding to suicide threats. If I felt he would commit suicide despite my words, I would of course have interrupted my sleep to get to him.

Joe was there in the afternoon. I promptly told him, "If you're going to act like a nasty little kid, I'm going to treat you like one." Then, inconsistent as this might have seemed, given his age and size, I took him over my knees and gave him a good spanking. He was acting like a child who threatens to hold his breath until he gets an ice-cream cone, and until he could face that incongruity, his childish activity would continue. Though his threat of suicide was a childish bid for attention and pity, when it appeared that he had really become aware of his need to change, it seemed all right to allow him to make a long session with a group.

In the session, we seemed to get no further, at first. Joe was beginning to upset the rest of the group, and one of them in particular was showing signs of stress and emotional exhaustion. At the time, I could see that Joe was feeling great anger, but, under the guise of being a nice guy, he was not being honest about expressing it. In order to contain him lest his anger erupt into violence that might hurt someone, I was holding him to the floor. When Joe noticed the effect he was having on the other person because of his own immature preoccupations, he cried out, perhaps in sheer frustration, "I'm going to get to him, and none of you will stop me." Giving in to his emotions, he flailed and struggled to get rid of me, completely oblivious of his own safety or of what people were thinking about him or whether he was doing the right thing. I contained his violence until he realized that he did not have to beat me into submission to get to the other person but that we could do it together.

Later he remarked to the group, "Now I know it is possible for me to reach out to another person. All these years I never knew I could do it, so I became wrapped up in my own trivial problems. Now I know I can do it." A group of peers, consenting freely to remain with him beyond the point of fatigue and apparent reason, were able to release the man hidden behind so much childish behavior.

LOVE AND MATURITY

What would we find if we really tore away the surface of our lives and exposed what lay beneath? We vacillate between the power and loving styles of life because our meager efforts to find out what we are really worth are seldom definitively satisfied. Most of us hesitate to probe too deeply. Rather than consider the possibility that we will find nothing, we leave the surface untouched and guess at what lies underneath or disturb it only slightly to take a cautious peek. Leaving the question of self-worth unanswered, we live a tolerable compromise as "good people" until the veneer is scratched and hints of corruption and violence begin to show through. Then we quickly polish over the rough places while we divert attention to more pleasing areas.

Freud used dreams to show what lay beneath. Through psychoanalysis, he uncovered sexual impulses with self-destructive potential. If we were to remove our defenses against them, a monster capable of all the atrocities and evils that men have unleashed on one another would be unearthed. According to Freud, once the monster was released it would eventually turn us on ourselves in a self-destructive rampage. It therefore seemed preferable to him to maintain an adequate system of defenses than to risk releasing the monster. In this compromise solution we release our primitive impulses only enough to prevent an explosion of bottled-up energy, but we control them sufficiently to prevent mutual destruction.

Freud's compromise is a capitulation to the power mode of living. Maturity in this mode is measured by the adequacy of controls and immaturity is revealed when controls are tenuous. Maturing becomes a process of building adequate defenses. To maintain intellectual control a person studies to increase his knowledge; to maintain his podium the teacher makes sure he knows more than his students; to command respect professionals hide behind their titles. Doctors and psychiatrists diagnose their patients and give labels to their conditions as a semblance of control over the sickness, as though to name a condition were to cure it. In the same way, diagnosing and labeling are ways to stereotype people and achieve power over them. By so doing we put them into a mold and are left free of the demand to discover them as individuals beyond what is contained in the

generalization. We gain control over them by catego-
rizing them, for in giving them tags we level their
individuality and make them common.

The Golden Rule Shows Tarnish

What we do to others in the power mode we also do
to ourselves. For fear of unmasking a vacuum we manip-
ulate ourselves to resemble others according to some
lowest common denominator. This way of seeking
safety from our primitive instincts to destroy, ravage,
and run becomes a process of leveling others and ourselves. Afraid that existence itself might be subject to
control and dependent on something outside us, we
even transform our God into an irrelevant power or a
fairy tale. If we can't control him, we deny him existence, so we won't have to deal with him. The power
mode eventually robs us of intimacy because we cannot
find value in ourselves to share with others, and every
human being becomes a potential enemy to be guarded
against lest he destroy us in our walled-in valley of
loneliness.

In the loving mode of existence, hiding is seen as an
indication of immaturity rather than a position of defense. Love itself becomes a continuum of honesty and
openness. When a man and wife continually renew
their commitment to each other, its meaning grows.
The words "I love you" never become a hackneyed
phrase to capture the marriage partner by making him
"feel good." Blind alleys of search become exciting
avenues of adventure as people sharing intimacy reach
beyond themselves in an ever closer approximation of

total union. No less real is the teenager's love with its
possibility of development. But it is a promising expec-
tation rather than an accomplished fact; there is hope
that honest search will be rewarded with increased self-
awareness and sharing.

When love is the mode of life, mistakes are not final
and unforgivable. Evil becomes reversible. But this can
happen only if two people can shed their armor and
expose themselves to each other totally. It can never
happen if we make of life a series of continual skirmishes
where each tries to master the other.

The ultimate impact of the power form of life is an
entrenchment in the impossibility of love. For love demands the truthful disarmament with significant others
in our lives. It implies a willingness to change and the
confidence that under fear and anger there is a core of
worth. It hopes that in a community of honest vulnerability, true affiliation can be discovered and enjoyed.
In this community affection can lead to love, hope can
be found in the objects that give rise to anger, and
courageous concern can rise above fear.

When man was created, he was unafraid and did
not hide. "Now both of them were naked, the man and
his wife, and they felt no shame in front of each other"
(Gen. 2:25). But when man tried to play for power, he
became afraid and his body was the symbol of his fear
that his attempt to master the ground of his being
would result in death.

The man and his wife heard the sound of Yahweh God
walking in the garden in the cool of the day, and they hid
from Yahweh God among the trees of the garden. But

> Yahweh God called to the man. "Where are you?" he asked.
> "I heard the sound of you in the garden," he replied. "I
> was afraid because I was naked, so I hid." "Who told you
> that you were naked?" he asked.
>
> (Genesis 3:8–12)

If in the power mode we have offended someone and are afraid, we must hide. Forgiveness has no place in power and we must protect ourselves. Ultimately we fear sharing ourselves with others lest we be controlled by them. Yet, if we had the courage to really be ourselves we would have the faith to follow the Person who emptied himself of his divinity in his attempt to share himself with us. We would have the faith to go beyond the fear with assurance that in us lives a valuable being who has but to reach out to share eternity with the source of his life. "We are to love, then, because he loved us first" (1 John 4:19).

In this sense then, sin is not an act, but a state of hiding, of refusing to grow because of our dishonesty, of closing ourselves off from loving contact with others. It is the shielding of our eyes with our hands to shut out the vision and invitation of Yahweh who wants, by his choice, to share himself with us and tell us what we are truly worth. Sin is the unwillingness to be open with those who love us, to come under their loving scrutiny. The result of sin is that we are caught in the quagmire of hiding and are sinking in the power mode of living. Our sin is the failure to transcend ourselves—to transform anger into hope, fear into faith, and to become vulnerable in love.

5

Therapy: A Microcosm of Life

PRECEDING chapters have explored the development of the human person in love and the various obstacles to growth. Frequent allusions have been made to marathon sessions and to various aspects of group therapy. This final chapter is my explanation of this approach in some detail and a brief description of my discoveries over the past several years. I begin with the origins and rationale of the therapeutic approach and then give a general idea of the extent of the work and the various risks and criticisms we have met along the way. While this chapter can hardly substitute for the more systematic investigation which I believe this therapy warrants, it should give the reader a general notion of its concepts and direction.

THE GENESIS OF MY APPROACH

About five years ago, after nearly a dozen years of practice in clinical psychology, I began to sense a keen disillusionment with the results of my work. I found that I could no longer carry on aware of the rising numbers of people in need of psychotherapy without making some drastic changes in my own approach to patients. Because I was seeing too many patients to be doing an effective job with any of them, I seemed to be wasting time—theirs and mine. I found myself growing more and more annoyed at patients who refused to improve for fear that the therapy might discontinue and leave them with no one to talk to. What I was beginning to discover was a depressing discontent with what I was doing to the lives of the people who came into my office.

At the same time, in my personal life, a general dissatisfaction began to fester under the surface. I had only partially come to terms with myself, preferring to seek refuge behind a time-consuming and absorbing practice. It was at this time that I was commissioned to conduct a seminar in psychology at a nearby major seminary for Catholic priests. In the first lecture, I revealed to the class my own search for a more effective mode of therapy. I also arrogantly announced my own religious agnosticism, based on some unfortunate and very unchristian responses from the churchmen with whom I had come in contact. It was too much bother to become an atheist, I told them, since such debates seemed to me meaningless academic muscle-flexing. There were more important things to do with my life.

When Dreams Crumble

Economically, professionally, and culturally, I had

achieved most of the dreams of the graduate student in psychology. I enjoyed the prestige of consulting positions on boards of education and mental health. I had an extensive practice, two university appointments, publications, a stable and enjoyable marriage, two healthy and bright children, and financial security. It seemed that I had everything the world could offer. But something was seriously lacking.

I began to have fantasies, about which I told nobody, of killing my wife and children and then committing suicide, so overcome was I by the utter hollowness of life and so confused about where to turn to preserve my family from the discovery of life as meaningless. These fantasies haunted me and so did the knowledge that I had seen the fulfillment of my dreams, and now there was no way to go but down. I could foresee riding the crest of life for another fifteen or twenty years, but then my humanistic power structure of success would slowly crumble and die. I was not a bad man nor was I a bad psychologist. I was not damaging my patients and in fact I had fostered in many of them an intelligent dislike for many of society's ills. But there had to be more to life than preoccupation with its diseases.

From Desperation to Hope

During my work with the seminarians I found I could no longer hide my unrest. My profession of religous indifferentism in such an obviously religious setting was really an urgent plea for rescue from a growing depression. I knew that I was lonely and without friends, except for my wife, and I began to sense a gnawing fear that if she were truly to know me, she would abandon me. It became clear to me that, while my structure of defenses was protecting me from others, it was totally inadequate to defend me from the questions I asked myself. I wanted to escape, and yet something inside me compelled me to search further.

Not especially hopeful—in fact, almost in desperation—I took the risk of slowly letting the seminary students know what was going on inside me. It was unfortunate that I could not reveal these things to my wife but had to reach out in a more "safe" situation. After all, if these men did not understand me or were to reject me, I could always retire to the security of my comfortable suburban life. And yet, I am sure that what initially inspired me to risk confessing my own fears and failures was the commitment to search for the truth which I had found in many of these seminarians. That risk, as it turned out, began a transformation of my life and practice, something so strange and fascinating I find it hard to believe at times. Rather than reject me for my theological antagonism and the immaturities and anxieties which I revealed to them, they began to talk to me—really to talk. They told me of their own loneliness, their own dissatisfaction, and their own failures to love —of many things they had never really faced themselves.

A Practical Solution

The following semester, when I began to have regular weekly meetings with a group of seminarians, the complacency and façades slowly began to melt as we revealed to one another our weaknesses and fears. We began to share the things that *really* made us angry, the things that *really* confused us sexually, and the things that we were *really* afraid of. In this, my first encounter in group therapy as more than a detached therapist, I received as much as I gave. The secret faults which each of us had feared would be a source of alienation from the others were becoming, instead, a source of strength and union. Isolation began to give way to dreams of freedom. Our relationships went from a desperate clinging for affection to a freely chosen decision to accept and share with each other completely. Discouragement and fear were being transformed into hope and trust.

In this setting I read the New Testament again, and for the first time began to realize the meaning of the words of St. John, "We ought to love one another because he loved us first" (1 John 4:10). I came to understand that the source of my being and my value did not rest totally within myself but rather in the fact that two thousand years ago a man had proclaimed that truth, honesty, love, and freedom were worth any price, and that he had sealed that commitment with his own death. At this point in my life I opted for the conviction that corruption is reversible, that hiding is stifling, that love is not only desirable, but possible.

I could not find any other language than this to express that love has become a possibility. If there is a need for a new morality it is the morality which teaches us the fellowship of the weak as a human possibility. Love then is not a clinging to each other in the fear of an oncoming disaster but an encounter in a freedom that allows for the creation of a new life. This love cannot be proved. We can only be invited to it and find it to be true by an engaging response.[1]

Confession Is Not Enough

It was gradually becoming apparent to me that self-confession was not enough. To reveal one's past to some significant person is truly a courageous step and can bring a good deal of insight. But something more was needed—a "corrective experience" to add credibility to the fact that the past need not control us, that we are truly free to determine our own future according to our convictions. Such an experience includes not only our own decision to change, but a commitment to others who will enlighten us when our perception is blinded, who will point up the inconsistencies in our life, who will *accept* us in our weakness and *invite* us to transform it into strength in complete freedom. This, I was discovering, was what Christ's life and message had been all about.

With this turning point in my life, I readily abandoned the medical model of psychotherapy with its underlying consumer mentality. Psychotherapy could no longer be something that someone purchased from me, or something I *did* to another. I could no longer consider my treatment successful if I helped a patient merely *adjust* to the world without a commitment to change those things in the world that are so ill-adjusted to the dignity of man. My relationships with my patients had to become increasingly more mutual—a sharing of convictions and failures, of virtues and sins.

What I have come to call disclosure-confrontation therapy was a natural outgrowth of my own life experiences and the self-understanding they brought. The technique of this approach is grounded in my own search for the truth and is not a gimmick gauged to push a person beyond where he wants to go. Disclosure-confrontation therapy has come to be more and more an *event,* an experience where a group of serious-minded, healthy people question themselves, open themselves to confrontation with others and respond, each according to the depth of his understanding and the strength of his commitments. It is an event terminating not in accomplished maturity or its appearances, but in a commitment to *grow.*

With this new insight into myself, I began to take a second look at those about me. It was clear now that my own marriage problems were not the result of bad faith or psychopathology, but of a lack of mutual sharing between my wife and me. And as I began to discover the lacunae in my own marriage and do something about them, I found I could help others to grow in their marriages. Instead of counseling a married couple in long series of clichés, I began to invite them to discover themselves and each other by self-revelation. This is the central meaning of the commitment two married people ought to make to one another.

It became more and more evident that in matrimonial difficulties the problems that were presented were not, in fact, the problems that should be faced. Impotence, frigidity, infidelity, hostility—all seem to mask a deeper fear as each partner questions, "What am I really worth?" I became more conscious that people were really hiding from themselves and from each other and that I could help them break down the walls of defense, if they would let me. I could help them find the strength that was there, if they would search for it. But they had to face the risk that their superficially healthy lives might be based on fraudulent premises. To face dishonesty has always been frightening, but in my experience it is well worth the risk and the pain.

The games of hiding played by teenagers became more transparent to me also. Captured by the consumer myth that life is for the *taking,* they are driven to "take" for their happiness. They are not able to respond or to be responsible. To respond is *not* to take, nor is growing up. The lamentable fact is that their parents, as the creators of the consumer culture, cannot lead their children beyond their own growth. Lacking the commitment to search honestly and openly for love, these same parents try instead to control their children, fearing to set them free where they might pry beneath the awesome masks and discover a weak and timid little wizard of Oz. Then the children, overwhelmed by lack of experience and insight, and yet disenchanted with their parents' lack of honesty, seek escape in sexuality, drugs, delinquency and suicide.

Finally, as a result of my own soul-searching, the crisis of the seminarians (and of all those committed to a clerical or monastic life) became more intelligible to me. Sincere men and women, attempting to build their lives around the message of the gospel, found themselves unable to adhere faithfully to the required discipline. Many of these individuals, as well as prominent lay leaders and other professed Christians, submerge their problem in protesting, in sexual affairs, or in study programs just to escape the unlivable conditions of community life. They avoid the frightening challenge of reexamining an institutional Christian Church which now teeters like a giant skyscraper about to leave the skyline and fall into the lake. I have found again and again that institutions are hopelessly inadequate substitutes for the lived reality of Christ's message; and conversely, that the angry energy directed merely at reforming or liberalizing the traditional structure is doomed to failure if there is not first a true commitment to that message.

DISCLOSURE-CONFRONTATION THERAPY

Gradually a growing conviction impressed itself on me that, for better or worse, we affect people with whom we come in contact to a much greater extent than we normally assume. From this, there developed a growing concern in my practice to focus less on the pleasure or comfort we derive from one another than on the mutual responsibility of knowing ourselves and sharing such insight. I began to view patients in terms of an immaturity-maturity continuum rather than to diagnose them simply as sick or healthy—and to emphasize the need for personal choice rather than to attempt the elimination of pathology. It became more important to deal with the dishonesty in a man's life than with the adequacy of his defenses. The question "What is wrong with my adjustment to the circumstances that seem to control my life?" was replaced with the questions "Where have I been? Where am I now? Where should I go?" Thus, the task of psychotherapy, as I have come to see it, lies in helping the individual to increase his responsible choices. How many of us remain immature out of fear of knowing who we are? We then transmit this fear to others and they in turn remain unwilling to discover their own value!

What was clearly needed, it seemed to me, was a human experience which would *correct* the damage and so restore the option for growth. This option would have to be based on the insight that behind the masks of daily living there lies beauty and not ugliness, freedom and not slavery, intimacy and not isolation. For if there is no way of healing the damage suffered in the past without denying it or hiding it, then we are doomed to be controlled and determined by impersonal forces beyond our capacity to endure.

Moreover, I came to understand that in our relationships with others, it is the *honest* community that should be fostered rather than the "healthy" community. For even though we tend to isolate those who are patently unhealthy, we do tend to encourage those who are dishonest to remain dishonest as long as they don't harm us or get close enough so that harming us becomes a real possibility.

If change cannot occur in a vacuum, then it is important to discover a situation in which a man can freely risk knowing himself because he is being accepted or rejected by others for what he really is. Not only is such a situation sadly lacking in many lives, it is often extremely difficult to create an environment in which openness can flourish. Essentially the rationale behind disclosure-confrontation therapy is the attempt to provide a group setting for corrective experiences and for demonstrating to individuals that love is not only desirable, but also possible.

If a man wants to know what he looks like, he must look at himself from every available angle. If he wants to know what his body looks like, he need only strip himself naked in front of a full-length mirror and observe. If the mirror is true, he will get an accurate image; if it is bent, he will see a distorted image. Unfortunately, the people around us who reflect us to ourselves tend to present a consistently distorted picture. When, for instance, people tell us that we are better or worse than others we believe them uncritically and we, in turn, project similar distortions to others whom we meet.

The only way a man can come to true self-understanding would be among people who are committed to honest and informed dialogue. Obviously, none of us can perfectly transmit such a totally unbiased reflection to another human being. But we can approximate it, and this is what disclosure-confrontation therapy aims at. If a group of people are willing to expend their energy to achieve such a mutual revelation, then the ideal can be reasonably approximated. If I choose to reflect intellectually, emotionally, and physically the impact you make upon me—and to open myself to a similar response from you—then our communication would be far more helpful than if I were merely to support you in your strengths and deal lightly with your weaknesses. If I were able to tell you of my anger without becoming violent, of my sexual feelings without seducing, of my fears without running, then we would be able to examine together the bases for these feelings in both you and me. When a group of persons committed to self-discovery so encounter one another, they will be able to correct past distortions and to make more enlightened choices in the future.

A Corrective Experience: Telescoping Growth

Disclosure-confrontation therapy is essentially a microcosm of life. It telescopes the normal growth process, by focusing on emotional attitudes that grow out of past judgments. When these emotional attitudes are misdirected, a new experience in a situation that arouses them but does not confirm them leads to their revision. It is a corrective experience. The group session forms a safe situation in which faulty emotional experiences can be corrected by being faced. It is in no sense a substitute for actual life, but opens new possibilities that can be applied outside of the group setting also. Honesty and growth are not prerogatives of an encounter group. The unfortunate reality is that most of us weaken in the face of life's pain and suffering and compromise for the sake of a carefree existence.

Ideally, of course, no special corrective environment should be needed. A man's dishonesties should be challenged within his everyday life and honest communication should not be qualified by the constant fear of rejection. This ideal is emphasized in our disclosure-confrontation therapy. It is our hope that once an individual has been helped by self-disclosure he might later be free to continue honest communication outside the group setting. In this sense, disclosure-confrontation marathons are grounded in the Christian promise that the truth shall set us free. For once a person has faced the truth about himself in a safe situation he is in a position to continue his growth in the choices open to him in his daily life. Feelings of fear, of anger, and of sex are neither good nor bad in themselves. They may be transformed into mature or immature behavior, depending on the prior commitments of the individual. Even the most integrated of us has to continue dealing with these feelings apart from a formal encounter situation.

The condition is never set that each member of the group accept every other member. A group member is committed rather to being open and honest, not to accepting and loving, since that choice can only be made freely after knowing and understanding the other person. The usual outcome of the sessions is, in fact, a community where love is given and accepted, but this is not the direct goal. Not every member is able to commit himself at the same level, although all are able to face themselves as they are.

In every group there are some people I like more than others. There are some I love more deeply. Though I cannot make a commitment to be fond of anyone, I can and do choose to remain with each one as he explores his own life for as long as it takes. I commit myself to share my feelings without exception or qualification—and I require the same commitment from each person who comes to the marathon session.

No guarantees are offered that anything will be accomplished in disclosure-confrontation groups nor is it implied that a person will feel better. He is not promised that he will learn about himself or become better. Yet the courage to continue in this approach comes from the fact that these results usually follow. I must emphasize that this form of group encounter is *not* a contrived technique geared to produce a specific set of responses. It is, rather, a new experience each time as we discover the uniqueness of each individual with his weaknesses and strengths.

To allow people to become part of an encounter group indiscriminately is hazardous and potentially harmful to the individual and to other members of the group. That this is frequently done in group sessions, I would suggest, is more an indication that those who organize the group fail to realize the depths to which a truly committed group can arrive than of their being indifferent or unprofessional. The groups in disclosure-confrontation therapy described here are carefully screened and selected on the basis of levels of maturity, self-understanding, stability, and interests.

THE MARATHON SESSIONS

The marathon sessions do not solve problems or undo damage. They expose the problems and the damage and clarify a person's options as he faces them. This kind of group therapy does not aim at producing a group solidarity which will disappear when the group disbands, but rather provides a type of individual therapy in a group setting which can, we hope, continue after the marathon is formally ended. Each person in the group focuses on a particular individual until that person faces himself, as he is, through the reflection of the impact he has on others. This is important, for a one-shot experience of openness could be harmful if it were to become a "happy memory" to console people in moments of depression and supply a standard against which the normal process of living is judged. For this reason I am reluctant to run a group session where the members will have to continue to be strangers to each other or unlikely to have much future contact. If a group cannot have the opportunity to deepen mutual understanding in future choices and growth, the marathon session will likely be an emotional kick which will eventually deteriorate into an unmeaningful memory. Love must find its fulfillment in the continual process of honest interaction with others.

As a general procedure, when an individual, for whatever reason, wants to confront a group in a marathon session, we take his case history and give him a number of tests (Thematic Apperception Test, the Minnesota Multiphasic Personality Inventory, the 16-Personality Factor Questionnaire, and a Sentence Completion Test). After the tests have been interpreted, at least one more interview is conducted in which the nature of the disclosure-confrontation session is carefully explained and the results of the test data are revealed. In this way, the chosen person is informed ahead of time what he might have to face on the session and the risks that he will most probably meet. But, more importantly, he is asked to make a personal commitment of honesty and openness, which I consider of far greater value than the testing itself.

The ideal size of the group is about eight. Fewer than six makes it difficult to form solidarity among the members and more than ten is simply too fatiguing for the group members and the therapists. There are usually at least two trained therapists, one of whom is a female if I am working with females. My wife has frequently participated in the sessions also. Moreover, I try as often as possible to have someone from a previous group present, e.g., a nun who has gone through a session to help with nuns, a married couple with married couples, and so forth. In this way, newcomers have the support of people who have been through at least one, sometimes several, sessions. Those who go through a session for the second time are there for a twofold purpose: to solidify their own gains and to share their growth with others with similar problems.

As Long As It Takes

The commitment of the group to stay together as long as it takes is critical. Marathons generally run about six days, though some have finished in three days while others have run as long as a week. Plenty of sleep is important, since we do not try to tire people into submission, but it sometimes happens that we must go beyond the point of normal fatigue for the sake of a particular individual. The session has no time limit so that the person encountering the group may truly have the opportunity to face himself completely and not be abandoned by the group before he has done so. An arbitrary time limit might leave a man with an unsolved problem.

Deliberate intellectual dishonesty is generally not

much of a problem during a session since the members know ahead of time that they may be expected to expose their past lives. Emotional dishonesty, however, is much more of a problem, since those who are ill-accustomed to expressing their feelings may unwittingly falsify them. Fortunately there are various effective techniques which can be used to help unmask what is being hidden.

The direct expression of physical aggression is never permitted between group members, but if such expression seems to be the only way a person can face his anger or fear, I do allow it to be directed at me. I am fairly well trained in the art of self-defense and can, in most cases, restrain a patient without harm to him or me. Several cases described earlier in the book bear out this fact. The risk of physical injury is never completely removed, but it can be reasonably minimized.

To participate in a disclosure-confrontation marathon, a person must see some need for change in himself and demonstrate a healthy dissatisfaction with his life. If he cannot make the commitment to change, I do not permit him to attend, since the lack of motivation would undermine the basis of the session. To place a person in a situation where it is unlikely that the group can help him to achieve maturity could create damaging frustration for the group members. A person must not only realize that change is desirable, but must be willing to sacrifice for such growth.

Most of the nearly eight hundred people who have been part of the marathons have been normal people eager to better themselves through self-understanding.

Among the groups that have attended marathons are adult men and women, clergymen, monks, nuns, high school counselors, teenagers, and university students. We have crossed racial, religious, and cultural boundaries within the group on several occasions. Recently, the approach has been extended to include patients with more severe pathological symptoms, though to date I have not handled brain-damaged patients, the elderly, the mentally retarded, or the very young.

The Individual's Symbols

While each individual generally suggests what techniques are to be used in helping him face his problems, there are certain characteristic procedures, all using symbolic actions to dramatize the level of growth of the individual. For example, if a person feels captured by someone in his life, he might be handcuffed to the therapist for as long as it takes for him to face his true feelings of enslavement. In each case, the person's consent is required. Essentially, whatever he is fearful of, he is asked to face, intellectually, emotionally, or physically, with due regard to safeguard his integrity. Thus, for instance, if a person is afraid of physical pain, it would be illegitimate for the therapist to hurt him. When the "real life" context cannot be met in the group setting, for whatever reason—physical limitations, moral consideration, or other—the situation can be handled through fantasy and imagination. Symbols are introduced only when feelings are hidden. By directing the imagination toward situations the person is afraid of, the therapist can lead him to play through and partially face the feelings involved. This should help him later to face similar situations in his real life.

Positive expressions of emotion are encouraged when they are spontaneous. For example, no one is ever *told* to embrace another member of the group, touch him, or demonstrate affection in advance of his own feelings. Whether such demonstrations arise from genuine affection or are merely contrived is generally evident to the group, so honesty and sincerity in such expressions is paramount. In our culture, where getting close to others physically is a strong taboo, especially among males, men are afraid to embrace their grown sons because it looks "queer." They are terrified of weeping in front of others because to be "weak" is unmanly. To see someone, in spite of these taboos, express an authentic emotion is rewarding, but to imitate such action without genuine feeling is artificial at best. The important thing about expression of love, fear, and anger is that they symbolize the breakdown of inhibitions, which in turn permits growth.

RISKS AND CRITICISMS

Because of the depth of the revelation and the severity of the confrontation, this method of encounter carries with it several serious risks, many of which have been alluded to. If safety alone were the criterion of success there could be no justification for disclosure-confrontation sessions. Although medicine has taken risks for many years in the cases of patients suffering from serious illness, we somehow assume that people who have been unable to find love in their lives are best left alone. We operate on the gross myth that time heals such ills, when in fact the sufferer merely gets used to them. I consider the risk of damage in disclosure-confrontation groups only slight when compared with the good that comes from an honest and loving life. To be sure, we must always attempt to minimize the risk, but never at the expense of isolating ourselves. What meaning can Christianity have in our own day if we accept only the promise of mercy, but ignore the great symbol of the cross which challenges the lover to be willing to risk his own life in the cause of love?

Of the approximately eight hundred persons who have been on marathon sessions, it was necessary to hospitalize only one man for a psychotic episode. The case is described in chapter 2. Since that time about ten other people have gone through psychotic episodes, but in each instance staying with them and refusing to be intimidated by the threat of psychotic behavior restored the person to a state of equilibrium and permitted the session to continue. For these people psychosis was a means of escape from a situation where they were asked to face the fears that they had successfully masked for so many years.

One suicide occurred following a session. While the death was tragic, it would seem to me an even greater tragedy not to have allowed the man an opportunity to face himself. It would undoubtedly have been *safer* not to have seen him at all, but that is true of anyone who agrees to come to a session. Although precautions can and should be taken, there is a point where you cannot predict how a person will deal with his life. It is sad that this man did not constructively deal with his, but I must also consider the many people whose attempts at suicide before coming for help have stopped after the marathon sessions.

Physical injury—seldom more than aches and bruises that disappear quickly—has occurred on sessions, even though efforts are made to avoid it. One man, who accidentally dislocated a shoulder during an outbreak of anger reacted to his injury with these words while in the hospital: "If only the problems of marriage were as simple as this pain. You can take the whole arm if it will help my wife and me and our children." Several months after the occurrence, this man still expressed no regret for having come to the session.

Another real danger is that group members might afterwards attempt to play "junior therapist" with their friends and neighbors. Without proper training and understanding, such attempts can cause serious damage. A few have occurred, and in one case a small group who had been through a session drove a man psychotic. We were able to help him return to normalcy, but we cannot overstress the danger of playing with other people's lives. Unskilled application of techniques can never substitute adequately for proper training and commitment.

There have been comparatively few who appear to be no better off after the session, not all of whom have even expressed regret at having wasted their time. As far as I can tell, other than the discomfort of living with others who have grown, none of them has suffered any mal-adjustment as a result of the session. Some have become extremely angry at me and have gossiped. The really unfortunate aspect of this is that it has discouraged some people from participating in our sessions who might otherwise have benefited greatly from doing so.

There is really no way to measure accurately the success or failure of disclosure-confrontation sessions in a way that will satisfy all criteria. Though we may have had more failures than those described here, the majority of people continue to keep in touch and characteristically report real growth in their own search for meaning and in the impact they are having on those around them.

Perhaps the greatest single criticism the disclosure-confrontation approach meets is that confidences are broken after the session. It is unfortunate that this happens. Sometimes a man is overanxious to share his experiences on the marathon and may unwittingly reveal aspects of another person's life. We do our utmost to discourage this, always indicating to members ahead of time that this is one of the risks that they may have to incur.

A very real limitation of these sessions is the level of maturity of the therapists. A man cannot lead another where he has not been first, cannot invite another to a level of freedom that he has not himself experienced. The therapist must always, therefore, face his own limitations and realize that blind spots in his growth may well be communicated to those whom he is directing. My own case, for example, has been helped tremendously through these sessions, but I regret the necessary and perhaps unhappy victims of my growth.

We have already dealt with the rationale behind

disclosure-confrontation and explained it as a tele-scoped life experience that is in no way intended to supplant other experiences. If such sessions were merely a weekend event, it could alienate the group from their respective environments. Our follow-up sessions and the data gathered to date strongly suggest that what has in fact happened is that the days spent together on a marathon become an opening to more possibilities for meaningful daily living. For really, nothing more happens in the marathon situation than a demonstration of the desirability and possibility of love.

The disclosure-confrontation session hopes to provide persons with experiences from which they can make a carry-over into their lives. It is not a refuge from life. Its goal is to help its members in their relations to the significant persons in their lives to become more truthful, more free, and more caring. A truthful relation is both open and honest—two different things that are both expressed in degrees. Unless they are distinguished, we may make the mistake of "revealing" ourselves to others by telling facts about ourselves without being honest about why we are doing so. We may sincerely but inadvertently heap burdens on others or hit them with our good-intentioned openness in a way we cannot know about and they are too frightened to tell us. A person may wear his heart on his shirt sleeve when it does not belong there. A parent may be open about his or her difficulties with a spouse, only to confuse and burden a child who is not equipped to deal with such openness. Revelation can frighten a person who is already too frightened to let us know what the revelation means to him. Honesty may take the form of "telling someone what we think of him" when it is neither asked for nor wanted. Thus our openness and honesty become weapons, tragically often wielded with the best of intentions.

When we use openness to capture another person, we jeopardize freedom. When we choose to let others know who we are and are able to let them respond to us freely without demanding their response, then it is clear that we also care about them. Freedom implies that we are responsible for the impact our lives have on others. The discovery of what this impact involves is a major part of the personal enrichment in a disclosure-confrontation session. In our ongoing lives, where we cannot know what this impact is unless others tell us, we are then left to our unfounded guesses.

The session, because of its intensity and open-endedness, presents ample opportunity to work out difficulties that prevent relations from being truthful, free, and caring. In our ongoing lives, such opportunities are often withheld or sporadic. The goal though remains the same. The way in which it is reached must be modified, however, since the particular "techniques" of a marathon session would be highly questionable in ordinary life.

Changing circumstances influence how open we can be and how much truth we can have in our relations to the various people in our lives. It is hoped that, with the significant persons, we can become increasingly truthful, essentially free, and deeply caring. Knowing when and how to develop these qualities in our daily relations requires great prudence or tact, in itself a virtue to be sought after. Even with those close to us, there may be a "moment" for truth, and we might need to wait for that moment. There is a *time* for everything, and openness out of its proper time can disrupt a relation which with waiting and respect for the moment could develop. As there is a time when we are ready to reveal ourselves, so there is a time when we are ready to respond in openness to another's self-revelation. As the soil is prepared before sowing, so there is a preparedness in others to receive what we have to say. This moment must be respected. Although more often we fail to let others know when they would truly hear, there is also the possibility of speaking painfully of ourselves when they are not ready to hear. Knowing the moment is dependent upon the intuitive rhythm of being human, for which rules are inept and risk is apparent.

AN UNCERTAIN FUTURE

"The evil that men do lives after them; the good is oft interred with their bones." Mistakes and failures in the process of the growing and applying the knowledge gained from a search such as this can often obscure the positive results. It would be presumptuous to predict that I might not in the future want to correct some of the things I have said in this book. I have not arrived at full maturity by any means, and the test of time will in all likelihood demonstrate to me more of my own blind spots. However, I feel there is sufficient positive evidence to warrant having shared these results of my practice and what I see as their theoretical implications. It is my hope that these insights will help others go beyond what we have already done.

In my own life, I find that even now the risks of discovery are still more frightening. But returning to the
easier, more comfortable power mode of life has lost its
meaning. I have come to see a definite direction in my
life and I have tried to share this with others without
imposing it.

For a long time I had little professional contact with
other therapists, except through reading. The personal
contact I did have proved to be disenchanting, but encouraged me to take my work along the lines outlined
here. As scientific studies are done and long-range
follow-up studies are made available, I hope to increase
contact with my colleagues. For as disclosure-confrontation becomes more widely known, I am becoming aware that I am far from alone in attempting to
discover a more meaningful approach to life and to
translate such an approach into an effective mode of
daily living.

Notes

Chapter 2

1. Sidney Jourard, *Disclosing Man to Himself* (New York: Van Nostrand-Reinhold, 1968), p. 47.
2. Eldridge Cleaver, *Soul on Ice* (New York: McGraw-Hill, 1968), p. 146.
3. Ibid., p. 148.
4. Jourard, p. 64.

Chapter 4

1. Henri J. M. Nouwen, *Intimacy* (Notre Dame, Ind.: Fides, 1969), p. 23.

Chapter 5

1. Nouwen, p. 36.